Working
Toward Success

OTHER BOOKS BY THE EDITORS

Making External Experts Work (2011)
Thriving as a Superintendent: How to Recognize and Survive an Unanticipated Departure (2013)
The Board and Superintendent Handbook: Current Issues and Resources (2015)

Working Toward Success

Board and Superintendent Interactions, Relationships, and Hiring Issues

Edited by Amy E. Van Deuren,
Thomas F. Evert, and Bette A. Lang

Published in partnership with the
American Association of School Administrators

ROWMAN & LITTLEFIELD
Lanham • Boulder • New York • London

Published in partnership with the American Association of School Administrators

Published by Rowman & Littlefield
A wholly owned subsidiary of The Rowman & Littlefield Publishing Group, Inc.
4501 Forbes Boulevard, Suite 200, Lanham, Maryland 20706
www.rowman.com

Unit A, Whitacre Mews, 26-34 Stannary Street, London SE11 4AB

British Library Cataloguing in Publication Information Available

Library of Congress Cataloging-in-Publication Data Available

Cloth ISBN: 978-1-4758-1552-8
Paper ISBN: 978-1-4758-1553-5
Electronic ISBN: 978-1-4758-1554-2

∞™ The paper used in this publication meets the minimum requirements of American National Standard for Information Sciences—Permanence of Paper for Printed Library Materials, ANSI/NISO Z39.48-1992.

Printed in the United States of America

Contents

Preface

Amy E. Van Deuren, Thomas F. Evert, and Bette A. Lang

The idea for this book originated from our dialogue and discussion on the pace of change in education and the belief that the changes should be addressed within a total framework of better understanding and improving board/superintendent relationships, partnerships, and interactions. As instructors in doctoral programs in two universities, we often hear about all of the competing interests practitioners face daily. Our primary reason for writing this book was to assist boards and superintendents to keep their focus on students.

We believe that if boards and superintendents had tools and content to examine, analyze, and work through changes together, the PK–12 system and students would benefit. We are aware that time and most economic resources are fixed and we stayed cognizant of these facts throughout the book. We focused on communication and relationships in the context of current issues to provide a resource that board/superintendent teams could use to work through the issues and improvements with renewed energy and commitment. How could we accomplish this goal?

In chapter 1, which is part I of the volume, we focused on the context, complexity, and leadership framework. Understanding the issues and roles the board and superintendent play in accomplishing the essential work of the district is critical if all leadership and organizational systems are to function efficiently and effectively. Three areas that are essential for functioning, high-quality board/superintendent interactions—content, connectivity, and relevance—helped organize our work. Because they are the glue that binds the contents of the book's chapters, it is worth taking a moment to unpack the context of each term.

Content is essential for effective dialogue and decision making. Board members and superintendents must be knowledgeable about a wide variety of topics in order to engage among themselves and with the community. While boards and superintendents do not necessarily need the same breadth and depth of knowledge on a given subject, they should share a common vocabulary and a deep understanding of foundational concepts. The chapters in part II are focused on currently relevant topics in education and set the stage for content depth necessary for effective dialogue and debate, and for reaching resolutions that benefit the district.

Connectivity is a catch-all term for several words used throughout the book that refer to communication and relationships, including partnerships, interactions, and teams. The ways that board members are connected to each other and the ways the board is connected to the superintendent significantly influence the level of productive decision making and the quality of the board/superintendent partnership. Fundamentally, connectivity is at the heart of effective board/superintendent relationships.

Relevance goes hand-in-hand with connectivity, in that when the board/superintendent team is well connected, the dialogue and issues discussed and debated are highly relevant to the academic success of students and the overall success of the district. Part III addresses hiring and focuses on hiring superintendents internally and externally as well as presenting information on hiring an interim superintendent.

As a handbook, the material herein is intended to create or promote renewed and/or continued focus on what is relevant to students, staff, parents, and the community. Our contributing authors have firsthand knowledge based on practical experience and theoretical underpinnings. Most of these individuals are current practitioners, and they have gone above and beyond the call of duty by giving their time, knowledge, and thoughtful reflection to share with readers.

We are very pleased to offer boards and superintendents suggestions for enhancing board/superintendent relationships, as well as creating greater understanding of hiring superintendents. Our contributing authors have a unique blend of practical experience and have conducted "applied research" in both areas.

Acknowledgments

We are indebted to the many students, parents, staff, community members, board members, and superintendents with whom we have associated during our journey in education. Thank you for teaching us so much and for your relentless resolve to make our schools better.

We extend appreciation to the school board members who willingly shared their opinions and insights for this book that we hope will become a useful resource to school leaders. Board members receive much criticism, little praise or remuneration, and keep showing up to fight the good fight for our students. Thank you!

We also thank the many current and retired superintendents who have provided us with valuable information and sage wisdom over the years. Superintendents have demanding, challenging, and rewarding jobs and strive to lead and manage while keeping a laser-like focus on student success.

We also say thank you to a group of unsung heroes in the world of PK–12 public education: administrative assistants. These individuals are deeply committed to the schools and districts they serve. Benjamin Franklin stated that "energy and persistence conquer all things." These words could be the motto of the talented and dedicated administrative assistants who support both people and processes in their daily work.

Thank you also to the special individuals who served as readers/reviewers and critiqued our book. Superintendent Wayne Anderson, former superintendent Kristine Martin, former board president Nancy Sonntag, and superintendent Ron Walsh all took time from their extraordinarily busy schedules to share insights and make this book more practitioner-friendly.

We extend a special statement of appreciation to the authors of chapters in this book. The writers, current and retired practitioners in school administration, have firsthand knowledge of both practical and academic considerations, which added richness, relevance, and depth to this book.

Next, we thank our friends and families for their support. This effort has been a significant undertaking and created periods of highs and lows. Those closest to us kept us pushing forward during difficult junctures. Onward.

Finally, we extend a special thank you to our trusted friend and colleague, Tom's former administrative assistant to the superintendent in the Janesville School District, Diane Wesner, for her efforts, patience, and skills. Thank you, Diane!

Amy E. Van Deuren
Thomas F. Evert
Bette A. Lang

I

BOARD/SUPERINTENDENT INTERACTIONS

Overview

Context, Complexity, and Leadership Framework

Amy E. Van Deuren and Thomas F. Evert

When the board/superintendent relationship works well, all parties understand the issues and the roles that each play in decision making, goal setting, progress monitoring, long-range planning and implementation, policy making, and creative problem solving. When roles and issues are clear, students and staff benefit. While the balance of power is inherently unequal because the superintendent serves at the pleasure of the board, the board relies on the superintendent for his or her knowledge and expertise in managing the operational and educational aspects of the district. References to the board/superintendent partnership recognize this imbalance of power and that teamwork is required for the success of the district.

When the board/superintendent relationship does not work well, the result can be detrimental to the district and to the community in a variety of ways. The negative media attention often causes tension and uncertainty among district personnel. Political mudslinging can take on a life of its own and takes attention away from issues related to schools, students, and education. District resources may be spent addressing issues related to the failed relationship rather than to issues benefiting student learning. In worst-case scenarios, the relationship is dissolved and the board is left to find another leader who they hope will be a better match or fit. These examples are just a few of the unintended negative consequences that can result from an unhealthy board/superintendent relationship.

The information presented in this chapter is intended to connect the dots for readers by providing general frameworks for consideration that illustrate some of the complexity of the board/superintendent relationship in today's educational landscape. The book is organized into four main sections addressing the board/superintendent partnership: (1) contexts and frameworks, (2) board/superintendent relationships, (3) hiring superintendents, and (4) in addition, a final fourth area lists all resources included in the book for ease of reference.

Part I comprises this chapter. It provides several overarching frameworks to structure board/superintendent content, connectivity (communication and relationships), and relevance. Other material in this book may be layered with the frameworks provided in this chapter.

Much has been written about the board/superintendent relationship; however, it is usually from either boards' or superintendents' perspectives, rarely considering both. The chapters in part II are intended to help boards and superintendents consider aspects of the relationship from both perspectives that may not always be obvious, such as the importance of helping a new superintendent learn the nuances of local culture.

Part III addresses a variety of issues related to hiring a superintendent. Arguably the most important appointment a school board makes is the superintendent. When presented with myriad choices for the position, including whether to choose an internal or external candidate or whether to hire an interim if the superintendent leaves at an inopportune time or with little notice, the hiring process can quickly become overwhelming.

We hope boards and superintendents find the content in this book useful as a starting point for open and productive dialogue. Whether you perceive that your board/superintendent relationship is strong or in need of attention, this book is an excellent point of reference.

FRAMEWORK 1: THE COMPLEXITY OF BOARD/SUPERINTENDENT INTERACTIONS

Board/superintendent interactions constantly change depending on the item or issue at hand, whether it is leadership, policy, or operations. These shifts in interactions can occur between individual board members and the superintendent or between the board as a whole and the superintendent. That is, sometimes the board and superintendent will be in agreement, while at other times there may be some level of disagreement between

Dimensions of
Individual and/or Entire Board/Board Member and Superintendent Interactions:
Leadership, Policy, Operations

Choose a person/entity and/or issue: Where is your relationship on the continuum? Where do you think others are?

Disagreement   Mid-point   Agreement

Figure 1.1.   Board/Superintendent Interactions

some, most, or all of the board members and the superintendent. The continuum of agreement/disagreement is shown in figure 1.1.

Interactions may be occurring with several board members and/or the entire board on numerous issues at the same time. When considering this fact, the inherent complexity of these interactions becomes obvious. More importantly, each of these interactions is an opportunity to build positive working relationships or, conversely, to erode these relationships. That is, the history of these interactions builds over time, and each interaction or set of interactions either builds or erodes trust, goodwill, and good faith, and affects future interactions.

Other factors affect the evolution of the board/superintendent relationship as well. New board members (and the loss of board members) create new dynamics among the board members and between the board and the superintendent. Significant changes in the law at the state and/or national levels can affect the natural flow and evolution of the board/superintendent relationship by launching everyone into uncharted waters. Drastic changes in the community, such as a major employer closing doors, can create new pressures on the board/superintendent dynamic that can add stress and tension to interactions.

FRAMEWORK 2: BOARD/SUPERINTENDENT PARTNERSHIP—CONTEXTS TO CONSIDER

Board/superintendent interactions can be contextualized in many ways, including: (1) the level of shared understanding, including role clarity, shared vision, and agreed-upon goals for the district; (2) the level of functionality of the partnership; (3) the balance of power and influence of each partner; (4) the ways that formal and informal rules affect functionality and decision making; and (5) the importance of establishing a good match or fit during the hiring process. Important considerations for successful board/superintendent tenure are inherent in each of these contexts, with each adding a layer of insight and understanding about the nuances of the relationship, which is anything but a "one-size-fits-all" proposition.

Role Clarity, Shared Vision, and Goals. General wisdom suggests that role clarity between the board and superintendent goes something like this: the board decides the "what" and the superintendent figures out the "how." That is, the board is primarily responsible for policy making, budget approval, program/initiative approval, and some level of progress monitoring on major initiatives. Many horror stories have been written about board members "micromanaging," that is, getting involved in the day-to-day operations of the district. While this rule of thumb is a good one, it is not always clear where the line is (or should be) drawn on a given issue. If role clarity were easily defined, it would not be such a pervasive problem in the arena of school district governance.

Establishing clear roles for the board and superintendent is a critical piece of the partnership. Not every board/superintendent partnership will define their roles the same way. The superintendent's leadership style, the experience and expertise of board members, and the issues up for consideration are all factors that the board and superintendent should consider when defining the role of each partner. In addition, roles may fluctuate somewhat depending on the issue and the amount of political activity in the community. Revisiting the role identification on a regular basis can help boards and superintendents maintain a balance of power that is appropriate for each position and that sustains the partnership.

Long-range planning, a shared vision, and regular goal setting are important tools for establishing role clarity and ensuring that all members of the board/superintendent partnership are in agreement on the big picture items. This foundational agreement will help the partnership weather the storms of inevitable disagreement and political tension that are part and parcel of leading a school district.

The Functionality of the Partnership. It is important that board members and the superintendent interact respectfully and in good faith with each other. Any party with an underlying agenda that contradicts shared vision and goals or otherwise acting to undermine efforts to serve themselves or harm someone else can significantly negatively impact the functionality of the partnership. Maintaining a functional board/superintendent relationship is the primary reason that it is important to cultivate a positive board image to attract high-quality, civically minded individuals to board service. A board/superintendent partnership viewed as dysfunctional can deter high-quality board candidates and attract agenda-driven candidates who may not serve in the best interest of the students.

The Balance of Power and Influence. Establishing role clarity, visioning, goal setting, and maintaining a high level of functionality help to ensure that power and influence among the board members and between the board and the superintendent sustains a healthy balance. The board/superintendent relationship does not work well when balance is not maintained. An overbearing superintendent does not get the necessary feedback and input from the board, and overbearing board members can stifle other board members or create undue tension. Maintaining a balance of power and leadership efforts requires that egos be checked at the door and that the board/superintendent team work in true collaboration, understanding that everyone in the partnership will have some decisions that will not go the way that they would like.

Formal and Informal Rules and Decision Making. Formal rules, such as Robert's Rules of Order, are commonplace for most boards. Knowing and using these rules effectively helps move discussion along and enables a fair process for decision making. Boards also establish their own informal rules that can govern many aspects of decision making, from where board members and the superintendent sit at board meetings to the order in which individuals are called on to make comments during discussion. These informal rules can make the decision-making process seem partial or impartial, depending on what the rules are and how they are implemented. It is worth taking some time to identify the informal rules that the board/superintendent partnership has established.

Establishing a Good Match or Fit during the Hiring Process. The importance of this aspect of board service cannot be overstated. No matter how extensive the interview process is, it is difficult to know whether a candidate might be a good fit for the district. It is also important for a potential superintendent to assess whether a district would be a good fit for his or her strengths. It is a courageous candidate who walks away from a lucrative position because he or she has a sense that it will not be a good fit. There is no magic formula for making the right hiring decision, but there is no question that there are as many different boards and superintendent candidates as there are school districts.

Considering these contexts, the board/superintendent partnership is obviously complex and the potential for pitfalls is ever present. None of these contexts of the board/superintendent partnership can be taken for granted, nor can they be counted on to continue over time; after all, board members and issues are ever changing. Being aware of these contexts and looking for signs of change that could signal problems are part of effective board and superintendent service. Maintaining a healthy partnership is critical for district success.

FRAMEWORK 3: FOUR LEADERSHIP QUADRANTS MEET SEVEN CONDITIONS FOR CHANGE

The board/superintendent partnership is critical to school district success. However, an agreeable relationship between the two entities is not the only criterion for success. Leadership and a clear understanding of the underlying issues are critical if the board/superintendent partnership is to facilitate improvements in student achievement. That is, the board and superintendent must be leaders *and* change agents in order to successfully move a district forward.

In 2000, the Iowa Association of School Boards (IASB), as part of its Lighthouse Study, compared six small- to mid-sized school districts (ranging from 1,395 to 5,163 students) in Georgia. Three were low-performing districts and three were high-performing districts. Each board had amicable relationships and was satisfied with their superintendent. A total of 159 individuals, including board members, superintendents, and school personnel, were interviewed.

Interview questions were based on seven critical conditions for change: (1) shared leadership, (2) continuous improvement and shared decision making, (3) the ability to create and sustain initiatives, (4) a supportive workplace, (5) staff development, (6) supports for school sites using data, and (7) community involvement (Land, 2002). Three major differences between high-performing schools and low-performing schools emerged from this study:

- *Belief in the Ability to Elevate Student Achievement.* Individuals in high-performing districts believed that they had the ability to elevate student achievement, while individuals in low-performing districts believed significant barriers limited their ability to influence student achievement.
- *Board Knowledge of Role and Influence.* School board members in high-performing districts understood the seven critical conditions for change and their own personal influence related to them. They could identify and describe school improvement initiatives and demonstrated understanding of their own roles in passage and implementation.
- *Shared Focus.* In high-performing districts, the school board and school personnel shared the focus on improving academic achievement, and both understood the linkages between school improvement initiatives and actions at the building and classrooms levels.

Critical components of leadership have been organized into four quadrants in figure 1.2. These critical components comprise the operational and instructional aspects of district leadership, acknowledge the impor-

Relationships	Analytical Skills/Instruction
• Shared Leadership • Shared Decision Making (and Continuous Improvement) • Community Involvement	• Supports for School Sites Using Data • Continuous Improvement (and Shared Decision Making)
Practical/Operational Understanding	Ideas/Change Agency
• Supportive Workplace • Staff Development	• Ability to Create and Sustain Initiatives

Figure 1.2. **Four Quadrants of Leadership**

tance of relationships, and recognize that ideas and change agency are necessary to move a district in a positive direction toward improved student outcomes. The Lighthouse Project's seven critical conditions for change are aligned with these four key areas of leadership. Note that the second condition, shared decision making and continuous improvement, appears twice in two different quadrants.

While some of these conditions for change, when combined with the leadership quadrants, may be associated more readily with either the board or the superintendent, the teamwork of both entities in the relationship is necessary for a high-functioning board. When considering change initiatives, especially on a large scale, such a model can provide a basis for reviewing the foundational aspects of the board/superintendent relationship and confirming role clarity before such change is fully underway.

CONCLUSION

The four sections of this book address issues of high relevance to board/superintendent teams, including various aspects of the board/superintendent relationship, hiring superintendents, and resources for board/superintendent teams.

While we have provided several frameworks that may increase understanding board/superintendent relationships, no single framework completely captures the board/superintendent partnership with all of its complexity and nuance. These frameworks provide overarching ways to conceptualize the board/superintendent relationship and can be used to focus conversations on areas of highest need. Superintendents answer to boards and the public, while boards answer to the public. This system does not provide a high level of oversight should the relationship start to go awry, so it is important that the board/superintendent team develop mechanisms to ensure that they are on track and in agreement regarding purpose, vision, and big picture goals for the district. This internal oversight is necessary in order to be high-functioning entities capable of decision making that minimizes political pressures and strives to provide the best education possible to the students being served.

REFERENCES

Iowa Association of School Boards (IASB). (2000). IASB's Lighthouse Study: School boards and student achievement. *Iowa School Board Compass, 5*(2), 1–12.

Land, D. (2002). Local school boards under review: Their role and effectiveness in relation to students' academic achievement. *Review of Educational Research, 72*(2), 229–78.

Ritsche, D. (2001). Wisconsin Briefs from the Legislative Reference Bureau. LRB-01-WB-4, January 2001.

II

BOARD/SUPERINTENDENT INTERACTIONS—PRACTICAL TIPS

2

Superintendent Behaviors and Influence on the Board/Superintendent Partnership

Michele L. Severson and Thomas F. Evert

Public schools in the United States have experienced an increasingly complex climate of accountability and demand for measurable results since the mid-1980s. This accountability culture has created, among other things, citizen unrest regarding public schools and an increased need for public schools to deliver PK–12 graduates who are knowledgeable, responsible, and skillful. State and federal politicians clamor for improvement and raise the achievement bar on a regular basis.

Within this context, school board members elected by voters and superintendents appointed by those board members must provide strong leadership in order to educate America's youth. The need for boards and superintendents to work together to promote PK–12 public education and garner support is unprecedented.

The importance of educational leaders having the trust of those they serve continues to be paramount in today's highly charged political environment. A unified approach to governance is founded on trust among the board, superintendent, and key stakeholders. The board and key stakeholders must trust the superintendent's leadership to get the job done for the district. The superintendent must trust that he or she has board and key stakeholder support.

Even though the board and superintendent work together as a team, each entity has unique roles and responsibilities. Board members act as a governmental body and each board member has no authority individually, while the superintendent is an "*n* of one." The role of the board is to hire, evaluate, support, and lead a superintendent, while the superintendent's role is to lead and manage the school district. Board members are typically lay people with expertise in areas other than education, while the superintendent is specifically hired for his or her expertise and experience in education. Finally, superintendents are typically evaluated on an annual basis by the board, while board members ultimately answer to voters every two to three years.

A united approach to school district governance has trust as its foundation for the board/superintendent relationship: "Collaboration, teamwork, and trust" have been described as "critical building blocks of leadership" (Burbach, Barbuto, and Wheeler, 2003, p. 4).

This chapter reports on research conducted to address the perceptions of four different behavioral traits closely related to trust by four key stakeholder groups: (a) school board members, (b) senior-level central office administrators, (c) teacher union leaders, and (d) Chamber of Commerce members. These stakeholder groups rated two superintendents recognized at the state level for their accomplishments in establishing positive relationships in their communities. The behavioral traits rated included resilience, integrity, decision making, and communication as identified by Reeves (2004) in his work on leadership assessment. Additionally, the two superintendents were asked to rate themselves on the behavioral traits listed.

The results of the study revealed that the two superintendents expressed positive ego strength by assessing themselves highly on each trait. The four stakeholder groups described the superintendent as having greater variability on each trait.

Based on the results of this study, we strongly believe that the more unified boards and superintendents are in dealing with the complex and difficult issues facing them, the greater the likelihood of success for students, staff, parents, and the community. A unified team approach means agreement on vision, mission, and goals, and also includes ample opportunities for dialogue and differences of opinion. However, once the board has decided on policy direction, it is necessary for both entities to move forward in a unified manner.

HOW TRUST IS FRAMED IN THIS RESEARCH

For this research, Reeves's (2004) model of multidimensional leadership was selected to compare the four stakeholder groups' perceptions of the superintendent with the superintendents' own perceptions of their leadership (school board members, senior-level central office administrators, teacher union leaders, and Chamber of Commerce members). Thus, collaboration, teamwork, and trust in the board/superintendent relationship were measured indirectly by focusing on resilience, integrity, decision making, and communication.

Resilience is a measure of emotional maturity and the ability to self-control. An individual with a high level of resiliency "admits failures quickly, honestly, and openly. . . . Once a decision is made, [the individual] fully supports enthusiastic implementation" (Reeves, 2004, pp. 106–7). This trait is important to the board/superintendent relationship because heated debate over controversial issues is part and parcel of the relationship, and both entities must have the freedom to disagree during the decision-making process. However, the board and superintendent need to come together once a majority board decision has been made so that the superintendent can implement those decisions with fidelity.

Integrity involves "meeting the letter and spirit of the law, [and] insulates the foundations of mutual respect for colleagues throughout the organization" (Reeves, 2004, pp. 108–10). Individuals with integrity actively seek differences in opinions and perspectives and meet commitments. While each member of the board/superintendent team may have his or her own desired outcome, listening to and soliciting differing opinions can help ensure the best decisions are made for the organization.

Reeves (2004) describes the importance of decision making as follows:

> Decision-making is neither by consensus nor by leadership mandate but consistently based on the data, vision, mission, and strategic priorities of the leader and the organization are visible, ingrained in the culture of the organization, clear and consistent evidence-based decisions that have been changed based on new data, all within the organization have the opportunity to meet one-to-one with the leader. (pp. 115–17)

Decision-making processes should take into consideration the culture and values of the community as well as available data. Stakeholder input is also critical to decision-making processes and should include individual meetings between stakeholders and leadership. The board and superintendent usually have a procedure in place for small-group or individual meetings between board members and the superintendent that does not violate open meetings laws. In addition, a mechanism for community input should be in place, especially for those decisions that will have significant community impact.

Communication is critical in the decision-making process and should include "clear evidence of parent and community-centered communication, including open forums, personal visits, extensive use of technology, surveys of parents and community. . . . [The superintendent's] calendar . . . [should reflect] numerous individual and small group meetings with staff at every level" (Reeves, 2004, pp. 117–18). Communication should be regular and ongoing and become ingrained in the culture and values of the community.

RESEARCH METHOD AND DATA COLLECTION

Research was conducted in two school districts that were nominated by state association directors. One director represented school boards and one director represented superintendents. The association directors were asked to nominate superintendents who were described as being effective at establishing positive relationships both within their district and within the greater community. In addition, the superintendents selected for this study had to meet the following criteria:

- He or she must have served as superintendent in the district for one to six years;
- The district population had to be between 1,500 and 3,500 students;
- The community had to have an operating Chamber of Commerce; and,
- The superintendent had to have made recognizable efforts at improving the school and community relationships.

Each superintendent was described as being a strong leader and was viewed in a positive manner according to two external sources. While

Reeves does not directly define trust through the use of a specific scale (nor does anyone else), we believe the four behavioral traits (integrity, resilience, communication, and decision-making processes) identified by Reeves indirectly address characteristics inherent in trust as related to leadership.

Research Questions. Three research questions formed the basis for this study:

1. How do members of each of the four stakeholder groups perceive the superintendents' areas of strength and weakness according to each of the four personal [behavioral] characteristics?
2. How do superintendents in this study perceive their areas of strength and weakness according to each of the four personal [behavioral] characteristics?
3. What are the relationships between the superintendents' and stakeholders' perceptions on each of the four personal [behavioral] characteristics?

Data Analysis. The first step in the data analysis was to calculate the mean perception score from each of the four stakeholder groups on each of the four leadership traits. Subsequently, the scores were compared between the two communities involved in the research. The final phase of analysis compared the superintendents' personal perceptions on each of the four traits with the mean perceptions from the stakeholders within their communities. By comparing the superintendent perceptions with other stakeholder perceptions, we were able to determine the level of agreement between the superintendents' self-perceptions and those of other stakeholder groups. From this data, we were able to make conclusions about the level of collaboration, teamwork, and trust inherent in these two board/superintendent partnerships.

The Reeves survey instrument grouped the traits associated with leadership into four behavioral domains (integrity, resilience, communication, and decision-making processes). The survey tool described in detail what each specific domain encompassed using four ordinal scale categories: exemplary, proficient, progressing, and not meeting standards. After reading the descriptors, the participants rated their superintendent on a four-point Likert scale. The ordinal portions of the survey were replicated from Reeves's (2004) original tool.

The scores from the school board members from each community were compared, along with the two administrative groups, the two union leadership groups, and the Chamber of Commerce organizations. Finally, the data were analyzed collectively to find survey agreement consistent between all stakeholder groups in both communities.

When the surveys were returned, the data were initially stratified by stakeholder groups within each community looking for agreement within and across group responses. This stratification provided a composite picture of each community involved. The second stage of analysis involved calculating the degree of convergence between the traits identified as strengths and weaknesses from the stakeholder groups in each community and the self-identified strengths and weaknesses of each superintendent. The degree of convergence between the stakeholder groups from each of the separate communities was calculated. The scores from the school board members from each community were compared, along with the two administrative groups, the two union leadership groups, and the Chamber of Commerce organizations. Finally, the data were analyzed collectively to determine the level of agreement between all stakeholder groups in both communities.

SURVEY RESULTS: FOUR STAKEHOLDER GROUPS' PERCEPTIONS OF SUPERINTENDENTS AND SUPERINTENDENTS' SELF-PERCEPTIONS

The mean scores for each of the four leadership traits were computed for each community subgroup (table 2.1). The traits were measured on a four-point Likert-type scale (4 = exemplary, 3 = proficient, 2 = progressing, 1 = not meeting standards).

The overall scores for the superintendent in Community A were positive as shown in table 2.1. Scores for resilience, integrity, and decision making were consistently proficient and moving toward exemplary. The lowest ratings were in communication from union leadership and Chamber members; however, these scores were just barely below the "proficient" level (still quite high). The mean scores for all stakeholder groups in Community A were compared to each other using a t-test. The t-test revealed that the two lowest ratings given by union leadership and Chamber members were statistically significant at the $p < .05$ level. This

Table 2.1. Mean Scores of Superintendent Behavioral Traits by Stakeholder Groups (Community A, Community B)

	Resilience		Integrity		Decision Making		Communication	
Community	*A*	*B*	*A*	*B*	*A*	*B*	*A*	*B*
School Board	3.4	3.2	3.5	3.4	3.5	2.5	3.5	3.9
Administrative Leadership	3.3	1.7	3.3	2.5	3.3	1.7	3.3	2.1
Union Leadership	3.1	2.7	3.4	4.0	3.3	3.0	2.9	3.0
Chamber Members	3.2	2.7	3.3	3.2	3.1	3.2	2.9	2.8

finding may demonstrate that those who work more closely with the superintendent perceive communication to be an area of strength as opposed to those who have less frequent contact with the superintendent.

The overall scores for the superintendent in Community B were lower than those for the superintendent in Community A, but were still positive. In Community B, the administrative team rated the superintendent consistently lower than the three other groups. School board members in Community B rated the superintendent lowest in the decision-making category. When the t-tests were performed on these stakeholder groups' results, the overall lower scores issued by the administrative team were statistically significant at the $p < .05$ level. Given that the scores from the administrative team were generally in the "progressing" range and moving toward "not meeting standards," it is likely that this superintendent was experiencing some significant internal challenges.

Table 2.2 represents the composite scores for each superintendent by behavioral leadership trait. Stakeholder groups' combined perception scores are reported for each behavioral leadership trait.

Table 2.2. Composite Score for Each Superintendent by Leadership Traits

Trait	Community	
	A	*B*
Resilience	3.4	3.3
Integrity	3.3	2.6
Decision Making	3.3	2.6
Communication	3.2	3.0

Overall, stakeholder groups were very consistent in viewing superintendent leadership traits. Integrity and decision making were the behavioral traits with the greatest variance between Community A and Community B. All composite scores were close to or over the "proficient" rating, with perhaps some area of concern for the superintendent in Community B in the areas of integrity and decision making.

Table 2.3 depicts how superintendents perceive their own strengths and weaknesses. Superintendents' scores are reported by each of the four traits.

Table 2.3. Superintendent Perceptions
of Strengths and Weaknesses by Trait

Trait	Community	
	A	B
Resilience	3.3	3.6
Integrity	3.6	3.8
Decision Making	3.5	4.0
Communication	4.0	3.5

The data in table 2.3 reveal that superintendents were consistent in rating their self-perceptions on each of the four traits. They rated themselves between proficient and exemplary in each area. These results likely indicate that the superintendents are confident in their work and believe their interactions with stakeholder groups are positive. These results may be indicative of strong ego strength and indicate strong confidence in their own abilities.

DISCUSSIONS AND SUGGESTIONS BASED ON RESEARCH RESULTS

The research revealed several important lessons for board members and superintendents. These conclusions, lessons, and "takeaways" are presented here by behavioral leadership trait followed by specific suggestions and ideas for board members and superintendents to use in practice.

Resilience. Both superintendents perceive that they are resilient. The stakeholders agree with superintendent A, but less so with superintendent B. Reeves (2004) indicates that resilience is a measure of maturity and the ability to self-control. Resilience is a personal characteristic that can be difficult for stakeholders far removed from daily operations to accurately assess. Those closest to the leader will understandably have deeper insight into the level of superintendent resiliency because they are present through more of the process pieces. Arguably many stakeholders will judge a leader's resiliency based on how they handle past organizational failures, either theirs or someone else's. High resiliency leaders are capable of successfully moving organizations forward through times of failure.

Integrity. Both superintendents placed a high priority on their personal integrity. Stakeholder groups also rated superintendent integrity high. Individuals with integrity meet commitments and actively seek differences in opinions and perspectives. Based on Reeves's definition, it appears that both superintendents and stakeholders understand the importance of integrity and believe that their district leaders possess this quality.

Decision Making. Both superintendents rated themselves very favorably in the area of decision making. With one significant exception, stakeholders confirmed this high (proficient) rating. One might speculate that stakeholder groups understand the critical role the superintendent plays in decision making and why a superintendent must make decisions. Decision-making processes, as described earlier, should take into consideration the culture and values of the community and available data.

Communication. Both superintendents rated themselves highly on communication and appear to understand the importance of communication in helping to deliver desired results. The superintendents believe they are excellent communicators. However, a clear finding of this research is that stakeholder groups believe superintendents must improve their levels of communication. Superintendents are often working hard to create opportunities and processes to better communicate with stakeholders. Perhaps it would be helpful to find new ways to assess the effectiveness of different avenues of communication.

IDEAS/SUGGESTIONS FOR SCHOOL BOARD MEMBERS AND SUPERINTENDENTS

As a result of our research, we submit the following ideas/suggestions:

A. *Superintendents*

- Resilience and integrity define who a leader is as a person; thus, these traits are less susceptible to improvement efforts.

- Structures can be put in place to improve decision-making skills. Specific decision-making models are available for boards and superintendents to consider (e.g., consensus model, shared decision making, recognition-primed decision model (RPD), site-based decision making). Boards and superintendents should agree on a model and use it faithfully.
- Superintendents must constantly evaluate their relationship with the central office administrative team. At times, a superintendent may perceive a higher level of team support than actually exists. A superintendent must never underestimate the role that central office administration plays in the ways a leader is perceived by all stakeholders.
- Superintendents should seek difficult, unfavorable feedback. Superintendents should not isolate or hear only from those who favor or support the superintendent's positions.
- Superintendents should strongly consider the following when seeking to improve communications with stakeholder groups: (a) provide data, (b) decision-making protocols, and (c) be open and honest throughout processes.
- Superintendents should develop a plan for communicating decisions to stakeholders. Request that boards clearly outline expectations for communication. That is, find out whether boards want regular updates on general progress or daily, hourly updates on happenings in the schools. Communication is arguably the most critical variable of the trust imperative as it relates to stakeholder perceptions.
- To address any gaps between the perceptions of stakeholders and superintendents in the four behavioral leadership traits, superintendents may seek feedback across all stakeholder groups, set their own professional improvement goals based on that feedback, and communicate the changes implemented to reach those goals.

B. *Boards*

- Boards should consider hiring superintendents who demonstrate successful indicators in all four behavioral leadership traits. While not always possible to define, these traits should be discussed with boards and superintendents and a working definition should be determined by the group.

- Boards and superintendents must practice resilience. There must be an understanding of the ebb and flow of district leadership. That is, there may be "high highs" and "low lows" depending on the issues at hand and the level of resistance from internal and external stakeholders regarding policies, practices, and initiatives.
- Boards must work with the superintendent and clearly establish protocols and parameters for decision making. When established, the board and the superintendent must follow the established process and communicate decisions with stakeholder groups at various times and in various ways.

CONCLUSIONS FOR BOARDS AND SUPERINTENDENTS

The following are conclusions for both board members and superintendents:

- It may be virtually impossible for a superintendent to communicate with a board frequently and clearly enough. Therefore, boards and superintendents must be clear regarding the system they choose to initiate, follow up, and monitor communication as regular practice. Multiple methods of communication are encouraged.
- Successful superintendents and board members place a high priority on their personal integrity.
- Boards and superintendents should strategically develop, implement, and revise a decision-making model to be used by key stakeholder groups (boards, union leaders, community leaders, and administrative team members).
- Superintendents must never underestimate the importance of support from their administrative team. Superintendents are encouraged to be watchful of how the team is communicating with other stakeholder groups.
- It is very important that superintendents and boards seek unpleasant news from stakeholders. Hearing concerns, problems, and disputes may be more important than hearing favorable feedback.

- Board members and superintendents must be resilient—that is, they must work together to enjoy school district successes and address district problems.

REFERENCES

Bass, B. M., and Stogdill, R. M. (1990). *Stogdill handbook of leadership: A theory and research* (2nd ed.). New York: Free Book.

Burbach, M. E., Barbuto, L. E., and Wheeler, D. (2003). *Linking an ability model of emotional intelligence to transformational leadership behaviors.* 46th Annual Midwest Academy of Management Meeting. St. Louis, MO, April 3–5.

Burns, J. M. (1978). *Leadership.* New York: Harper and Row.

Northouse, P. (1997). *Leadership: Theory and practice.* Thousand Oaks, CA: SAGE Publications.

Reeves, D. (2004). *Assessing educational leaders: Evaluating performance for improved individual and organizational results.* Thousand Oaks, CA: Corwin Press.

Severson, S. (2011). *Perceptions of superintendent behaviors that influence relationships with key stakeholders including board members.* Doctoral dissertation. Madison, WI: Edgewood College.

3

School Board Professional Development

Amy E. Van Deuren

Effective school board governance does not happen by accident (Land, 2002). Whether referred to as "high-impact" boards (Eadie, 2005), "high-functioning" boards (Walser, 2009), "moving boards" (LaMonte, Delgardelle, and Vander Zyl, 2007), or high-quality boards, school boards that function with the best interests of students and learning in mind while being responsible stewards of district resources can have a positive impact on their district and community. These successful boards interact effectively with one another, the administration, and stakeholders and focus their efforts on student learning and academic achievement while checking personal egos and agendas at the boardroom door.

An important part of purposefully moving boards toward achieving high-impact board status involves professional development for board members. Few individuals are elected to a school board knowing the ins and outs of board service, including understanding open meetings laws, the differences between the role of the board and the role of the administration in school district management, the etiquette and expectations for participation at the board table, and school district finance. In short, many new board members must learn the intricacies of board leadership.

With increased urgency for measurable results and higher accountability standards in recent years, new board members are often plunged into their new leadership roles with little time to learn and reflect before being asked to make decisions and vote on major and minor initiatives and/or policies. More than ever, it is important that new and existing board members engage in professional development to ensure that they are all working from an agreed-upon set of rules and policies (although opinions will certainly differ!) that will enable productive disagreement and a foundationally sound process for decision making reflecting the values of the community and the district and serving students well.

THE NEED FOR BOARD PROFESSIONAL DEVELOPMENT

Board professional development is an important opportunity to learn, reflect, and grow in a context created specifically for learning. Whether the professional development is held in open session or small, nonquorum numbers engage in sessions at different times, professional development provides opportunities to ask questions and learn about aspects of board service not necessarily tied to a particular agenda item or initiative.

Professional development should be part of the board's culture. There should be an expectation that regular and ongoing learning opportunities for board members will be provided and that board members are interested in becoming better board members. Cultivating a culture of learning at the board level sets an excellent example for the rest of the district and encourages healthier within-board relationships and board administrative relationships. In addition, establishing a culture that embraces ongoing professional development for board members clarifies the values of the board to the community and can generate interest for school board service among high-quality candidates.

Van Deuren (2012) conducted a survey of 272 board members in Wisconsin using a survey tool that included both closed-ended (forced choice) and open-ended (narrative response) items. The results revealed that most board members (89 percent) were indeed interested in professional development opportunities on some aspect of board service. Only 11 percent indicated that they were not interested in professional development. Board members were asked about several aspects of professional development, including identifying (a) which subjects and topics were of highest interest to board members, (b) which subjects and topics were most needed to help the board engage in productive dialogue and make better decisions, and (c) ways that boards would prefer professional development be scheduled and structured for greatest impact. The results of this research will be discussed in detail in this chapter and are intended to provide some insight into what board members are thinking as they contemplate their own needs and resources (time and money) for professional development.

SUBJECT AREAS AND TOPICS OF INTEREST TO BOARD MEMBERS

Board members were asked early in the research to identify one of three overarching subject areas or categories of interest in which they believed that they needed professional development: (a) interacting with other board members, (b) the role of the board, and (c) aspects of the school district. Board members most often responded that they were interested in various aspects of the school district (45 percent). Next, they were interested the role of the board (26.2 percent). Lastly, board members were least interested in professional development having to do with interacting with other board members (8.8 percent).

Included in the study were open-ended items in which board members could indicate broad subject categories and specific topics of interest to them that did not appear in the study. As a result of these open-ended items, a new category of professional development was added: "school and/or district improvement." When this category was added to the other three options stated in the paragraph above, it essentially split the "aspects of the school district" category into two subcategories: (a) aspects of the school district and (b) school and/or district improvement. The numbers in the other categories remained essentially the same on the open-ended responses as they were on the closed-ended responses.

Figure 3.1 shows the categories that were defined in the study and the specific topics of interest that board members selected most often in each category.

Most board members chose aspects of the school district as their preferred category for professional development. Those respondents were most interested in anything to do with finance or budgeting and long-range planning and goal setting. Other topics of high interest included hiring effective teachers and other employment issues and referendums.

Those respondents who selected school and/or district improvement as their preferred professional development category were fairly evenly divided among the following topics: (a) innovations in education; (b) issues

Categories	Aspects of the School District	School and/or District Improvement	The Role of the Board	Interacting with Other Board Members
Topics	(a) Finance and budgeting (b) Long-range planning and goal setting (c) Hiring and employment issues (d) Referendums	(a) Innovations in education (b) Issues and trends in education (c) Community engagement and ownership (d) Technology, new curriculum, and teacher development	(a) How does board policy affect student achievement (b) Legal obligations of board member (c) Board/superintendent role clarity	(a) How to work with other board members and deal with board conflict (b) Communication skills

Figure 3.1.   Categories and Topics Selected as Most Interesting by Board Members

and trends in education; (c) community engagement and ownership; and (d) technology, new curriculum, and teacher development.

Those respondents who selected the role of the board as their preferred professional development category were most interested in the topic of how board policy affects student achievement. The legal obligations of board members came in a distant second. Board/superintendent role clarity was the next most interesting topic, while using data and other accountability measures were also identified as topics of interest.

A small number of board members indicated that they were interested in the category of interacting with other board members; those members indicated that they were most interested in learning how to work with other board members and deal with board conflict. Communication skills were also identified as a topic of interest in this category. While this category was identified as a high priority among few board members, study results indicated that when the board members are not interacting effectively with each other, then higher-level decision making for the benefit of the district suffers.

Interestingly, board members also expressed distinct opinions about those professional development opportunities that they would *not* want to attend. Ninety-four of 272 respondents provided answers to this item. Twenty-nine percent of respondents indicated that they would be uninterested in attending professional development on the topic of working with other board members. The responses under this category were particularly pointed. Phrases including "team building activities/games—HATE THEM!!!!" and "I'm not interested in 'I'm okay, you're okay' smarmy crap" were included in these responses.

Other professional development topics that board members indicated were of low or no interest included the following:

- Classroom discipline
- Voucher programs
- Homosexuality inclusion
- Response to intervention
- Insurance seminar
- Diversity issues
- Technical aspects of the law
- Legislative issues
- Topics that outline another district's success
- Sessions about how hard a teacher's job is
- Day-to-day operations more appropriately handled by district staff

This list is interesting in that a superintendent can find out a great deal about what board members are thinking and what they value by asking them about what topics they do *not* want to address in professional development. So often the board is asked about what they *do* want (e.g., communication, information) that the "don't wants" are left to be inferred as a byproduct of getting to the "wants." Given that board professional development cannot be mandated, it is as important to know what boards are not interested in studying as what they choose to study.

Ultimately, there is no one-size-fits-all solution in terms of professional development topics of interest to board members. The choices for professional development would appear to be dependent upon how close a board is to being high functioning. That is, if a board is having issues of board members working with other board members or clarifying the board/superintendent roles and responsibilities, these board members tend to be more interested in addressing these issues first. A board that is working well together is likely to be interested in learning about various aspects of the district, that is, knowledge necessary for effective decision making. Those boards whose members are savvy and knowledgeable are likely to be more interested in school/district improvement,

where they are empowered to make decisions that are calculated to positively impact student achievement.

WHAT SHOULD PROFESSIONAL DEVELOPMENT LOOK LIKE?

Structure. On this point, board members were clear in their responses. In
the context of board professional development, board members are adult
learners who want to be actively engaged in their learning. Interactive
learning was selected by 205 of 272 board members (75 percent), and 151
of those responses (74 percent) indicated that workshops with breakout
sessions were the preferred delivery method.

Based on the forced-choice and open-ended responses, the message
from this survey was clear: most board members want different professional development than that which is typically offered; that is, the
traditional lecture method, usually accompanied by a Power Point presentation. Interaction with the professional development providers and
other participants and engagement in the learning process are critical
components of adult learning.

Expertise. As a group, board members indicated a definite preference
for professional development providers outside of the district rather than
receiving professional development from district administrators. Board
members as a whole indicated that the state board association was an
effective source of board professional development (69.1 percent, $n =$
188). Private consultants were also considered an effective source of
professional development, although not necessarily the *best* source of
professional development (77.6 percent, $n = 211$). When board members
were asked about consultants, they were asked not to consider costs,
only effectiveness.

Given this information, superintendents and board members should
seek out professional development opportunities that utilize available
resources from state board associations and consultants, if budgets allow.
Professional development offered by district personnel may be viewed
more skeptically and as less reliable than professional development from
outside sources. The implications of these results indicate that board
members want a fresh perspective from their professional development
opportunities rather than the status quo. Perhaps workshops and sessions

offered by district personnel are not perceived as professional develop-ment; rather, these opportunities are part and parcel of learning about the district and how it functions.

PRACTICAL CONSIDERATIONS
FOR PROFESSIONAL DEVELOPMENT

When contemplating board professional development, there are several practical aspects of resource allocation to consider. First, board mem-bers must be willing to devote extra time to attend professional develop-ment opportunities. Second, boards and superintendents must determine whether members have the interest and ability to travel. Third, boards and superintendents must know the board members' preferences for scheduling. Fourth, boards and superintendents should ascertain the degree to which board members are comfortable with technology and whether technology-based learning opportunities are a practical option. Finally, it is important to assess a board's willingness to allocate funds to professional development.

Time. Almost three-quarters of board members indicated that they were willing to spend time on board-related activities, and well over three-quar-ters of board members indicated that they were willing to spend extra time on board professional development. Board members' ability to allocate time for professional development does not appear to negatively impact decisions on whether or not to attend board professional development.

The data reveal that the type of district in which a board member serves is a factor affecting the willingness of a board member to allocate time for professional development. Rural board members are significantly more likely to be willing to allocate time for professional development than suburban board members. Both groups indicated a high degree of willing-ness to allocate time for professional development; however, rural board members were even more likely to do so.

If time proves to be a real obstacle for some board members, the board may wish to employ a modified "train the trainer" model. That is, selected board members may attend certain professional development sessions and then report back to the board during a regularly scheduled board meeting. This approach has the added benefit of informing the community of the board's work in self-improvement and promoting a positive image as an engaged, learning board.

Travel. Board members were somewhat split on their willingness to travel for board-related activities, although almost three-quarters of board members indicated that they would be willing to travel to attend professional development activities. Board members' willingness to travel for professional development does not appear to negatively impact decisions on whether or not to attend professional development opportunities.

The data reveal that age may be a factor that affects the degree of willingness to travel. Board members aged fifty-six and over were most willing to travel for professional development, while board members aged twenty-five to forty were least willing to travel. Only slightly more than half of these younger board members were willing to travel for professional development.

Several factors may contribute to this difference in willingness to travel by age group. Younger board members may have jobs and/or families with children that preclude easy travel. The extra expense, time, and effort required for travel may simply be more difficult for these younger board members. Other factors, such as the cost of travel to the district, may also be a concern for some of these board members. The bottom line is that travel is an issue on which board preferences and abilities may vary greatly.

Scheduling. Board members indicated a strong preference for scheduling regular board activities separately from professional development. That is, instead of having fewer, longer board sessions during which activities are combined, members preferred more frequent meetings and sessions of shorter duration. Data indicate that board members do not want to be overwhelmed with too much information or too many agenda items at one time and would prefer to schedule sessions with fewer agenda items.

Data indicate that age and years of board service may affect tendencies regarding scheduling preferences. Older board members (aged fifty-six and over) and those with over ten years of board experience were significantly more likely to prefer more frequent, shorter sessions than younger board members and those with less than two years of board service.

Younger and/or newer board members are often learning the breadth and depth of board service. The time commitment required to execute the responsibilities of the office is significant. It can be tempting for boards to try to be efficient with everyone's time (including the board clerk who must post the meeting notice) and schedule professional development on the same night as a board meeting or committee meetings. While some members are able to sustain interest and attention for a long period of time, more likely than not, most board members will prefer to schedule professional development in separate sessions during which they can become deeply engaged with the subject matter and material at hand.

Technology. Over three-quarters of board members indicated that they had a high level of comfort with technology-based learning. Data indicate that most board members are familiar with and able to use technology-based learning formats. A lack of knowledge about technology precludes a relatively small percentage of board members from engaging in professional development presented using a technology-based platform.

Not surprisingly, data reveal that nearly one-third of board members aged fifty-six and over were not comfortable with technology. Board members aged twenty-six to forty were the most comfortable with technology, with only slightly more than 10 percent indicating that they were not comfortable with technology-based learning. That is, older board members are almost three times more likely to be uncomfortable with technology-based learning. Webinars, online learning, and self-directed modules can be efficient, cost-effective learning tools if board members are able to take advantage of them. Being aware of the technological abilities of board members is an important factor to consider when assessing professional development options.

Funding. Over three-quarters of board members indicated that they supported allocating funds to discretionary activities in general and board professional development in particular. However, data reveal that several factors may affect board members' willingness to allocate funds for these activities.

District size was a significant factor in willingness to allocate funds for board professional development. Board members in districts with 1,001 to 2,000 students enrolled were more willing to allocate funds than board members in smaller districts with less than five hundred students. In addition, board members in districts with 1,001 to 2,000 students were almost twice as likely to allocate funds for professional development than board members in districts with more than ten thousand students.

Age was also a factor in board members' willingness to fund board professional development. Board members aged fifty-six and over were almost 20 percent more likely to support funding professional development than board members aged forty-one to fifty-five. In addition, board members aged twenty-six to forty were over 30 percent more likely to agree that the district should *not* allocate funds for professional development than board members aged fifty-six and over.

Years of board service were also a factor affecting willingness to fund board professional development. Board members serving for over ten years were 25 percent more likely to allocate funds for professional development than board members serving for less than two years.

These differences present important considerations for boards and superintendents as they develop a board professional development plan. Very small districts have small budgets and costs for professional development are typically not prorated by district enrollment; therefore, it costs more of the total budget to allocate funds for professional development than in larger districts. Large districts (more than ten thousand students) have larger budgets; however, many are experiencing significant budget shortfalls that may preclude a high level of comfort with funding board professional development. In addition, larger media markets may have more outlets to publicize (and therefore criticize) board expenditures on their own behalf.

Data reveal that older, more experienced board members are more willing to allocate funds for professional development than younger, less-experienced board members. Perhaps longer tenures of board service and life experience create a sense of value and need for board professional development. The old adage "the more you know, the more you know you don't know" comes to mind. Perhaps, too, more experienced board members have had time on the board to take advantage of the professional development offered at low or no cost and they are willing to invest financial resources in order to engage in new and meaningful experiences. It is interesting that less-experienced board members, who arguably need professional development the most, are the least willing to allocate resources for it.

SUMMARY

An important trait shown by effective boards is their commitment to and engagement in professional development activities that help them to become better board members and to increase their knowledge base as they address a wide variety of challenges in their districts. Research was conducted to determine what board members wanted from professional development in terms of interests, needs, and preferences in several areas. These areas included content, delivery, and practical considerations.

Board members prefer content that is relevant and relates to various aspects of the district and district improvement. They prefer a delivery method that is interactive and keeps them engaged with the provider and other participants. Regarding practical considerations, most board members are willing to spend time, allocate funds, and travel if necessary to attend professional development opportunities. In addition, most are comfortable with technology-based learning options.

Board members have a good idea of what they want and need for their own professional development, including the topics they wish to see addressed, the instructional delivery method, and the practical considerations that make it all feasible. When planning professional development, the board and superintendent should take all of these factors into consideration to make a professional development plan that is customized to be as impactful as possible.

REFERENCES

Eadie, D. (2005). *Five habits of high impact school boards.* Lanham, MD: Scarecrow Education.

LaMonte, H., Delagardelle, M., and Vander Zyl, T. (2007). *The lighthouse research: Past, present and future: School board leadership for improving student achievement.* Des Moines, IA: School Boards Foundation, Information Briefing, April 2007, vol. 1, no. 9.

Land, D. (2002). Local school boards under review: Their role and effectiveness in relation to students' academic achievement. *Review of Educational Research, 72*(2), 229–78.

Van Deuren, A. (2012). *School board member needs and interests regarding the content, structure and delivery, and other considerations related to school board professional development.* Doctoral dissertation. Milwaukee, WI: National Louis University.

Walser, N. (2009). *The essential school board book: Better government in the age of accountability.* Cambridge, MA: Harvard University Press.

4

Board/Superintendent Dynamics and Interactions

Amy E. Van Deuren and Thomas F. Evert

Interpersonal relationships and the larger contextual framework of interactions between and among board members and the superintendent are a critical component of a healthy and functional board/superintendent relationship focused on student learning and big picture long-range planning goals. Much of the writing and research starts with the board/superintendent relationship and places it in the context of the school district. This chapter focuses on the board/superintendent partnership and explores what each person in the partnership brings to the table to facilitate communication and decision-making processes, which have long-term effects on a school district.

When considering ways to focus on these relationships and interactions, our research and discussion started with a focus on the effects of one board member on the rest of the board and the superintendent. We spoke to several superintendents who had experienced firsthand the way in which one board member can exert extraordinary power and influence, often resulting in an imbalance of power among board members and eroding a shared decision-making model.

Numerous articles and personal accounts recall the adverse effects that a highly skilled, political, manipulative board member has had on boards, superintendents, and the community. This board member seemingly has the innate ability to influence, steer, and direct the board and/or superintendent in a way that seems to result in this board member getting his or her way much of the time. However, it soon became clear that the actions of a single board member did not take into account the rest of the board and the superintendent and the qualities that they brought to the group relationship.

The superintendent is in a unique position in the board/superintendent partnership. The superintendent is often referred to as an "*n* of 1" due to the fact that he or she occupies a uniquely defined, highly visible, and ultimately accountable role in the district. While this definition of the superintendent's role captures much of the responsibility inherent in it, we were not convinced that had been addressed beyond personality variables or that it had been studied in a complex or comprehensive manner regarding what it means to be an "*n* of 1" in the context of the board/superintendent relationship.

As the search for a framework for this discussion that would prove useful to both boards and superintendents, we then focused our attention on models that would identify function and dysfunction within board/superintendent interpersonal relationships and contexts. The purpose of working out such models was to discover if there was a way to (a) make better sense of the complexity of board/superintendent relationships and (b) provide a framework for changing dysfunction in the board/superintendent team in a way that encouraged self-reflection rather than finger pointing.

The first model that we considered was a traditional "family therapy system" model, which focuses on the alliances of family members in relation to one another and describes various roles family members can play at various times within the system. An example of an unhealthy alliance in a family system may be where one spouse communicates with and relies too much on the advice and company of a child as opposed to communicating richly, frequently, and honestly with the other spouse. Standard examples of roles family members in dysfunctional families can play at different times include the hero, rebel, enabler, clown, and lost child (Schilts, 2006).

There were several reasons that we set aside the family therapy system model. First, while these roles could certainly be very useful in understanding and describing some board/superintendent interactions, they were not sufficient to capture the complexity of the board/superintendent dynamic. Second, board/superintendent team members are not blood relatives and do not have the in-depth history that family members have with one another. Third, family are not elected to their "chairs" at the family table like board members are, nor are they appointed to their position like a superintendent. Finally, family are not constrained by open meeting laws regarding how and when they can meet and how many may meet together at one time without posting a public meeting notice.

After much dialogue, our research and discussion led us to the models presented on the following pages. This work was extremely challenging because it gets to the heart of who we are as either board members or superintendents. It is affective and very personal, and it takes enormous courage and a willingness to be vulnerable in order to look in the mirror to evaluate how our interpersonal interactions are affecting the entire team. It takes even more courage to do something about our behaviors that may be negatively impacting the district.

THE LAYERS MODELS

An interesting way to consider the contexts of board/superintendent relationships is to conceptualize it in layers. That is, even in a public position, our "public persona" is made up of different combinations of our professional and personal selves, depending on the situation and company. Alliances and friendships in the workplace can evolve between colleagues as individuals shift their interactions over time from addressing the business at hand to discovering shared values, beliefs, and personality traits. That is, the better we get to know each other, the more we know what a person is really about, and this knowledge can help us learn to interact better with each other.

Communication Layers. At any given time, a variety of communication layers may be at work between and among the board/superintendent team. Depending on how transparent these layers are to other members of the team, various layers of communication can either help identify relevant issues and concerns or work behind the scenes to undermine and obfuscate the most visible layer of communication at play at the time. The interaction of these layers of communication can work synergistically to build trust or drive an initiative or implementation forward or they can work against each other to create inertia, inaction, distrust, and misplaced focus on peripheral issues.

Each organizational team must define its layers of communication, which will depend on the roles of the members and the opportunities for one- and two-way communication that each member has available.

In general, more layers of communication involved between and among board members (both formal or informal) usually results in a higher likelihood of dysfunction and frustration among the board/superintendent team.

One way to frame common layers of communication contexts that board/superintendent teams frequently experience between and among themselves is shown in table 4.1.

The context column titles the context of the communication, which can occur between or among any board/superintendent team members. Almost always (unless in closed session), the board will be present together in a publicly visible context. The description column provides an example of characteristics that may be part of the communications that occur under this label. Each board/superintendent team may characterize their communications in these contexts (if they engage in them) a little differently.

The last column identifies professional or personal self characteristics. Interestingly, more inherently covert communication contexts (exclusionary alliances and coalitions) lend themselves to more personal expressions of communication. That is, people are generally more comfortable letting their true feelings be known (and letting themselves be vulnerable) in smaller groups with less public exposure. They often share opinions and ideas that they would not share with the larger group, or "try it out" with their smaller group of trusted colleagues first before speaking to the entire board/superintendent team.

Coalitions and alliances among small, nonquorum board members cross the line from collegial support to inappropriate communications when those communications involve plans and action steps to influence the outcomes of the entire board/superintendent team by leveraging an unfair advantage gained by their alliance or coalition. That is, while it is not necessarily a bad thing to talk things over with a board colleague, it can be all too easy to slip into the bad communication habits of dysfunctional boards.

The most successful board/superintendent partnerships focus on the communication that takes place in open and closed session with the full board and in small groups that are transparently known (at least not hidden) from other board/superintendent team members (layers 1 and 2). These board/superintendent teams minimize or simply do not engage in layer 3 or layer 5 communication (exclusionary alliances or coalitions) and do not express ideas and opinions with individuals on the board/superintendent team that they would not be willing to express to a larger audience.

Table 4.1. Board/Superintendent Communication Layers Model

	Context	Description	Professional or Personal Self Characteristics
Layer 1	Public persona	Communication and personas displayed at public appearances. This communication is typically formal and polite. Individuals purposefully cultivate the persona displayed in layer 1 contexts.	• "Best foot forward" • Polite and formal • Opinions often carefully considered with regard to political impact
Layer 2	Small group discussion	May be public or behind the scenes, and where discussion is often more direct or heated among two or more people in the board/superintendent team. This level of communication is openly known to all (or at least not hidden) and an important part of the decision-making processes.	• More informal than layer 1 • More open forum for dialogue and debate • May or may not feel comfortable expressing true feelings • Still transparent • Can positively impact layer 1 communication
Layer 3	Political coalitions	These communications involve influential board members (with or without the superintendent) agreeing on outcomes and actions prior to a board meeting or full board discussion. This layer of communication typically results in outcomes being decided and/or driven in a particular direction prior to a public meeting. This communication is often more covert and may or may not be communicated to others on the team.	• Usually high level of personal comfort • Likely to be more honest about desired outcomes and concerns • May say things that he or she would never say to the whole group • More likely to engage in personality discussion about other team members • Likely to adversely affect layer 1 and 2 communication

(*continued*)

Table 4.1. *Continued*

	Context	Description	Professional or Personal Self Characteristics
Layer 4	Outside advocates	This layer adds additional complexity and influences into the communication process. An example of using outside advocates effectively would be to engage key community members in discussions about passing a district referendum. An example of using outside advocates to undermine an initiative would be to solicit key community members to write letters to the editor advocating against a district initiative when you have not made your position clear on the issue. Depending on the circumstances and transparency in which outside advocates are included in the decision making, the board/ superintendent team communication responses can range from highly functional to highly dysfunctional.	• Can be highly professional or highly personal, depending on context • Can result in building successful coalitions and advocacy partners to move the district forward • Can be used with equal power to undermine and sabotage support for district initiatives and implementations • Adds a complex layer of new communicators to the board/superintendent team when brought in at the board level • Can enhance or sabotage layer 1 and 2 communication
Layer 5	Exclusionary alliances	Members of the board/ superintendent team handle disagreement on an issue by not talking, stalling the issue, and generally halting productive communication. These exclusionary alliances often result in significant dysfunction and frustration among board/superintendent team members.	• Are often personal in nature • Can be indicative of deeper underlying issues with the board/ superintendent partnership • Professional, courteous communication is low or nonexistent • Usually negatively impacts communication at layers 1 and 2

Successful board/superintendent teams carefully consider outside advocates at critical junctures when agreed upon by the team. Outside advocates are not merely stakeholders giving input. Rather, these are "special access" individuals who are invited into layer 1 and 2 communication. The district may formally hire individuals, such as an independent hearing officer for expulsions, the district's legal counsel, or a financial consultant, or they may be volunteers solicited to support a district initiative on behalf of the board/superintendent team.

Of course, changing layer 3 and layer 5 dynamics, if they exist, is easier said than done. Such impetus for change cannot come from the superintendent or one board member alone; rather, a desire and commitment to operate on layers 1 and 2 must exist within the majority of the board/superintendent team. It is incumbent on each board/superintendent team member to make a commitment to layer 1 and 2 communication so that they will not find themselves inadvertently involved in layer 3 or 5 communication. Layer 3 and 5 communication may seem like nothing more than political "hardball" at first, but it is the stuff that dysfunctional boards and "revolving door" superintendents are made of.

Decision-Making Layers. Perhaps less complex but still worth consideration are the layers of influence that comprise the contexts and interpersonal relationships with regard to decision making. Decisions are not made in a vacuum, and board members typically do not reach their final vote on an issue without careful consideration and input.

On most boards, there is a distribution of power and influence. That is, some board members often hold more sway over the board/superintendent team than others. This influence may be the result of political savvy, time and effort spent on a certain issue or in a certain area, or a special skill that the board member brings to the table, such as the ability to ask key questions or make particularly cogent arguments for his or her position.

How board members exert their influence during the decision-making process speaks volumes about what they value and whether they honor the views and opinions of their colleagues. It also largely determines how empowered the board/superintendent team feels as a whole to engage in a productive and lively decision-making processes that result in outcomes that benefit the district and community. Table 4.2 shows one example of the way board/superintendent teams may organize themselves, either purposefully or not, to engage in decision making.

Table 4.2. The Decision-Making Layers Model

	Context	Description	Influencers
Layer 1	Public board	The board as viewed by the media portrayal to the public and visible at board meetings	• Citizen input • Media • All other interested internal and external stakeholders
Layer 2	The working board	Those most involved in the decision-making processes, often behind the scenes	• Some board members most of the time • Some board members some of the time, depending on the issue • Those usually willing and able to spend the most time unpacking and working through issues
Layer 3	Kitchen cabinet	Strong supporters of other board members or the superintendent and/or board members who communicate frequently with the superintendent and/or board president	• This group is most likely to generate interest in an issue or initiative from the board team • Enables the board president and superintendent to stay on top of the "pulse" of the rest of the board • Not always most vocal in public board meetings
Layer 4	Outside influencers	Other leaders, such as union presidents, politicians, clergy, and business leaders	• Can have significant influence on specific outcomes • Usually issue-specific involvement • May have an agenda or desired outcome that either aligns or conflicts with the board/superintendent team • Important for long-term district support among the community

	Context	Description	Influencers
Layer 5	Changing alliances	A board may experience typical alignments on certain issues, where most votes come out a certain way (e.g., a seven-member board may usually have 6–1 or 5–2 votes). However, on certain unique or critical issues, the board vote may be more closely split down the middle and can go either in favor or against the issue (e.g., a seven-member board may be 4–3 or 3–4 on a sensitive or critical issue)	• Some issues may trigger different decision-making mechanisms within individual board members (e.g., political capital) • May be indicative of healthy board engagement and consideration of each issue • May be indicative of underlying problems or erosion of board support for the superintendent

The decision-making layers model is set up like the communication layer model, except that it is usually healthy to have all five layers present in a successful board/superintendent partnership. Providing the board/ superintendent team with a variety of contexts in which to be actively involved in decision-making processes keeps board members well informed and deepens understanding about the ways that decisions made at the board level impact student achievement.

Engaging in planning and decision-making processes outside of the public meetings of the full board does not thwart the transparency of the political process. Rather, it ensures that necessary debate and discussion are framed in ways that accurately capture the issues most relevant to the board and community. Selected members of the board (not a quorum) and administration, including the board president, superintendent, and directors, often do the difficult work of figuring out what questions to ask in order for the board to have the information they need to make decisions. This work typically happens outside of the regular board meetings.

The issue of alliances is critical in board/superintendent team interpersonal relationships and contexts. Many boards will often vote a certain way as a "default" on many issues. While such a default can be handy for superintendents in the vote-counting process, it also creates an equilibrium that can be significantly shaken when a sensitive or critical issue arises that tests the political mettle of board members.

That alliances shift is not in itself an issue; it is healthy for board members to align differently on different issues depending on their values and the manner in which they choose to represent the community. It is why alliances shift in some decision-making processes that is more important. If all members of the board/superintendent team are maintaining fidelity in their communications, then the arrangement of alliances should not adversely affect decision-making processes. However, if the board/superintendent team is functioning (or *dys*functioning) across several layers of communication, then alliance shifts are often a key signifier that the board/superintendent relationship is not working well.

These models provide one way for board/superintendent team members to consider the level of transparency that they exhibit between and among each other as they engage in communication and decision making. Open meetings laws and the need for governmental transparency create contexts for interpersonal relationships that often seem at best contrived and stifled and at worst become a dysfunctional power struggle.

An important aspect of board/superintendent relationships involves each member being aware and mindful of the interactions in which he or she is involved. At the very least, board/superintendent team members who take the time to be reflective leaders should at least gain some insight into their own motivations for board service and the way that they manifest the authority and responsibility of their position.

While the layers models do provide an interesting context for considering certain aspects of board communication and decision making, the models are decidedly complex and lend themselves to many permutations to consider when attempting to gain further understanding of board/superintendent dynamics. This complexity eventually leads to a formula in which each interaction increases the total interactions significantly (i.e., seven board members x one superintendent x two issues x three outside influencers = forty-two possible combinations of actions).

Probably most damaging, though, is the "bad faith actor," be it a board member and/or a superintendent, who does not care that they are not a "team player." These individuals can wreak havoc on a district. Using the layers model to identify what can happen if bad actors act badly can only diagnose; it does not offer solutions to fixing what is likely not fixable.

THE THREE Rs

Another more positive way to frame board/superintendent relationships and contexts focuses on three broad aspects of these interactions: (a) *reasons* individuals run for the board and become superintendent; (b) *responsibilities* board members and superintendents face; and (c) *roles* board members and superintendents can play in these interactions.

If board members and superintendents were to increase their understanding of the three Rs, it may result in better decision making and communication that could only benefit students, the district, and the community. If the media and/or public would also increase their understanding of the three Rs, communication, and decision-making processes, it may result in a more informed citizenry and support for an improved system of public education.

The First R: Reasons. There are likely as many reasons why individuals run for the school board or become a superintendent as there are individuals currently in these positions; however, common reasons for seeking leadership positions have been identified in research.

A recognized expert in the area of board service is the late Dr. Donald McCarty. During lectures at the University of Wisconsin–Madison in the mid-1980s, Dr. McCarty spoke about the reasons that individuals run for the school board.

One group of individuals was attracted to board service by the desire to do good work and promote the public good. These individuals professed a deep commitment to the democratic process and the American way of life. A second group was interested in politics and wanted to learn firsthand about the ins and outs of local politics, thinking that board service might be a stepping stone for another political office at the local or state level. Board members in this category may have interest in eventually running for city council, state assembly, or the state senate.

Finally, McCarty described individuals who possessed a wide range of motivations and concerns. However, the common denominator is that these individuals focused their candidacy on one primary issue, such as seeking additional funding for a program, a desire to add or eliminate a particular program, or the desire to remove someone in the district from their position.

An important aspect of McCarty's research acknowledges that a board member's motivation could change over time after a number of years of service. For example, a board member who initially ran for the civic good may shift his or her focus to seeking other elected positions after five years of service.

Perhaps the category with the most significant change after some time of board service was the single-issue board member. Once elected and board service was underway, this group of individuals learned how much work was involved. As a result, some of these individuals did not seek reelection after one term. Others learned to like the complexity of board service, enjoyed the learning and homework necessary for success, and went on to become board members serving for the civic good.

Martin, Johnson, and Lay (2002) found that superintendents also shared many common reasons for engaging in district-level school leadership. The top three extrinsic motivators for men serving as superintendents included salary, peer/mentor encouragement, and the variety of responsibilities involved. The top three extrinsic motivators for women serving as superintendents included peer/mentor encouragement, location of the position, and salary.

Martin, Johnson, and Lay (2002) also looked at intrinsic motivators for serving as a superintendent. The top three intrinsic motivators for men included the superintendency as a step toward career goals, professional reputation, and the ability to impact education. The top three intrinsic motivators for women included the ability to impact education, the ability to initiate change, and personal satisfaction.

As might be expected, board members and superintendents typically do not overtly voice their deep-seated reasons for engaging in district-level leadership. However, these reasons for engaging in leadership provide valuable context that can help all board members and the superintendent understand each other better. While we do not advocate that everyone clearly state their motivations for everyone to hear (that would be an amazing board/superintendent team, indeed!), we do suggest that being aware of the most common reasons that individuals engage in these leadership roles can help all board/superintendent team members understand and empathize with each other more effectively.

The Second R: Responsibilities. A great deal of information is available about the responsibilities of boards and superintendents in the district.

State statutes, national, state, and local school board policy statements, vision and mission statements, and job/duty descriptions define the responsibilities of the board and superintendent.

With all of the information available, board members still continue to seek clarification about their responsibilities. Basic board responsibilities include:

- Promoting the common good to be obtained by having an educated citizenry;
- Being responsible stewards of public funds, including setting and monitoring the district budget;
- Determining appropriate policies for the district ranging from curriculum goals to hiring practices to field trip permissions;
- Ensuring that relevant laws are followed in the district, for example, number of school days, curriculum standards, and expulsions;
- Hiring and evaluating the superintendent with the goal that the superintendent "leads" the district in terms of implementing board policies and regulations.

The superintendent advocates for student achievement, learning, and success. The superintendent is responsible for communicating with the board regarding the need for and implementation of board-approved policies. The superintendent generally develops an annual budget for the board to modify, if needed, and to approve. The superintendent also recommends the hiring of specific staff subject to board approval. The superintendent is responsible for establishing a district climate that fosters student success and growth.

Typically, a board will ask that a superintendent be a visible advocate for public education and specifically for students in the district. It is important for boards and superintendents to communicate regularly to ensure that there is agreement on the role of the superintendent in terms of advocacy, leadership, and goal setting.

The responsibilities described above do capture the basic aspects of board and superintendent responsibilities, but anyone who has served in either capacity knows that these responsibilities only scratch the surface. The responsibilities of the board and superintendent regarding their interactions with each other seem somewhat less clear; however, research provides valuable insights into the responsibilities that board/ superintendent teams take on in order to engage open communication and fair, authentic decision-making processes.

Alsbury (2014) stresses that boards should be discouraged from micro-managing administration and instead focus on governing for high student achievement. He advocates for consideration of a balanced board governance model that sets high expectations for and monitors student learning. Alsbury stresses that boards need to be knowledgeable about the means to reach the student learning goals they establish.

Shifting some of the board focus from an operational lens to an instructional lens increases board understanding about the goals that the district is trying to achieve for students and helps the board/superintendent team determine what policies, programs, initiatives, and resources will move the district toward these goals.

The Third R: Roles. Board members are elected and superintendents are appointed to fulfill different roles; however, these roles can become blurred depending on community values, individual agendas, perceived needs, and other considerations. Typically, board members are tasked with policy making, budget approval, setting tax levies, hiring and evaluating the superintendent, and similar types of duties. Superintendents are tasked with managing all operational and instructional aspects of the district in partnership with the administrative team and district stakeholders.

A critical part of the board/superintendent partnership is constant communication to ensure that role clarity is always defined, updated, and adjusted when appropriate. Enoch (2013) provides several "messages" that can serve as effective sounding boards for both board members and superintendents to initiate such communication:

- Conversation 1: *Superintendents and boards should never violate closed-session confidentiality as it is illegal and destructive.*
- Conversation 2: *Both superintendents and boards should attend to finance issues, be good stewards, and be willing to make difficult decisions.*
- Conversation 3: *The board should limit its personal involvement in evaluation to one employee: the superintendent. When needed, the superintendent must explain to the board that serving multiple masters is problematic.*

- Conversation 4: *Superintendents must remind the board not to "shoot the messenger" and work with boards to develop the capacity to expect the unexpected. Promote an open exchange of communication and ideas.*
- Conversation 5: *A superintendent and board must master how to respond to complaints from staff and the public. Each must learn that it is important to show interest and empathy without indicating automatic agreement. Both must direct a complaint to the lowest level in the organization where the answers can be found. From time to time, superintendents should remind boards about what things are working well in the district.*
- Conversation 6: *Boards should be encouraged to create and enforce thoughtful policies. Policies should clarify core beliefs held by the board and superintendent. Policies that allow exceptions are guidelines, not policies. Each party, the board and superintendent, must learn the difference.*

Bhimsack and McCabe (2013) articulate seven highly effective practices of board members. These effective practices are sage advice for superintendents as well and so are worth repeating for the benefit of the entire board/superintendent team.

- *Going Solo Is a No-No:* The board is a body of members and the superintendent is an "*n* of 1" in the district with a team of support and a board team to lead the district. Going solo tends to have undesirable consequences for everyone, whether it's the board or the superintendent doing the soloing.
- *Respect the Team:* Personal attacks, bullying tactics, and political grandstanding hurt the individual and the board/superintendent team. Team members will not (nor should they) agree on many things, and working through disagreements in a respectful manner will ultimately result in a better outcome for the district.
- *Understand the Difference Between Board and Staff:* Role clarity for board/superintendent teams is critical. When boards get involved in management issues, it erodes their ability to hold the organization accountable for outcomes. A clear general division of leadership duties between the board and superintendent in which the board leads

in the goals and policy arena and the superintendent leads in the daily management arena sets a solid foundation for a successful board/ superintendent relationship.

- *Share and Defend Your Views, but Listen to the Views of Others:* Engaging in debate and disagreement is an important mechanism for working through issues and arriving at the best outcomes for the district. The board/superintendent team's success can be largely measured by the ways in which they handle conflict and disagreement. Board/superintendent teams should maintain a professional demeanor (never make it personal) and avoid bullying techniques, such as monopolizing the discussion or saying the same thing over and over when the desired response is not received.
- *Do Your Homework and Ask Tough Questions:* The board/superintendent team makes critical decisions that can affect the district for years into the future. Expressing legitimate concerns and asking tough questions can help the district avoid future pitfalls resulting from poor decisions or direction.
- *Respect Your Oath:* Personal agendas, politics, and power can negatively impact the good intentions of board/superintendent team members. Remembering who the team serves and why the team exists in the first place can keep all members grounded and acting in the best interest of the district and community.
- *Keep Learning:* District leadership is challenging and exciting, and the context of education is constantly changing. Regardless of experience, there is always much to learn. Seeking out formal and informal learning opportunities benefits the individual and the board/superintendent team.

A Final Thought for Self-Reflection. Johnson-Morgan (2011) identifies over twenty dysfunctional character types in the context of nonprofit leadership. These character types are an excellent tool for self-reflection, dialogue, and professional development. They can apply equally well to board members or superintendents. Here are twelve character types that most closely apply to board members and superintendents.

- *Dictator:* Does not seek advice; does not encourage expression
- *King/Queen:* Seeks advice, then recommends his or her own agenda

- *Machiavelli:* Is a strategist who often pulls the rug out from others; others cannot tell what he or she is thinking
- *Playwright:* Scripts every scenario and assigns roles to other members; quickly jumps in when the dialogue goes off script; acts as the "director" of the play
- *Executive Director "Wannabe":* Tells other board members he or she could do better than the current board president or superintendent
- *Skeptic:* Questions all communication, strategic plans, and initiatives; abstains on votes and second guesses decisions
- *Expert:* Has an opinion on everything and shares it freely; tends to dominate the discussion
- *Bomber:* Likes to create a stir, often throwing a bomb into the dialogue or process that creates confusion
- *White Rabbit:* Always late, does not prepare but always appears busy, and leads board to dead ends
- *Big Daddy:* Overinflated sense of importance; likely a local hero; takes important calls during meetings
- *Absentia:* Not present much and makes virtually no impression on fellow board members; yet somehow keeps getting reelected
- *Historian:* Been around forever and can recall every decision. Will tell everyone that proposed initiatives have already been tried and failed, and will tell everyone how things have always been done

CONCLUSION

Board/superintendent partnerships are complex and challenging entities to describe and discuss without resorting to the problems and stereotypes often associated with them. Experts remind us that the best way for board/superintendent teams to function effectively is to clearly articulate roles and responsibilities and interact in a professional manner that encourages discussion and debate while setting aside personal agendas. We know that board/superintendent teams that maintain open communication and work well together are generally successful decision makers.

While personal agendas, politics, and power are real factors that boards and superintendents must address in their own leadership, Huffington (2014) identifies an additional metric perhaps as powerful in driving successful board/superintendent partnerships, which is worth consideration as a parting thought: individuals have a need for well-being, the use of wisdom, feeling worthy, and understanding the importance of giving. These needs are well served by engaging in district leadership and do not conflict with doing what is best for students, staff, parents, and the community.

REFERENCES

Alsbury, T. L. (2014). Jefferson County Public Schools: Shaping the future. 2013 School Board Quality Standards Report.

Bhimsack, K., and McCabe, T. (2013). 7 practices of highly effective board members. *American School Board Journal, 200*(7), 21–25.

Bind, L. (2013, July 6). A new era for school boards. *Milwaukee Journal Sentinel,* Milwaukee, WI.

Carlson, L. (2013, August 6). School board wants greater control over message, district administration. *Marshfield News Herald,* Milwaukee, WI.

Caruso, Jr., N. D. (2013). Board savvy superintendents: Help the board take its own temperature. *School Administrator, 70*(6), 11.

Enoch, S. (2013). Board savvy superintendents: Conversing courageously with your board. *School Administrator, 70*(11), 11.

Huffington, A. (2014). *Thrive.* New York: Harmony.

Johnson-Morgan, E. (2011). *Dysfunctional characters often sit at the board table.* Leesburg, VA: Nonprofit Risk Management Center.

Kennedy, D. C. (2013, May 31). WASB director explains what makes a healthy school board. *Daily Press,* Ashland, WI.

Martin, B., Johnson, J., and Lay, M. (2002). What motivates individuals to become leaders in public and higher education? *Professional Issues in Counseling.* Retrieved from http://www.shsu.edu/piic/spring2002/indexspring02.html.

Moscinski, D. (2013). Self-fulfilling prophecy. *American School Board Journal, 200*(6), 14–15.

Schilts, G. W. (2006). *Guy'd Lines—Rules for living from my 30 years as a psychotherapist.* Janesville, WI: Crossroads Psychological Services, LLC.

5

Variables That Affect the Complexity of Board/Superintendent Interactions

Thomas F. Evert and Bette A. Lang

The importance of clear and regular board/superintendent communication has been discussed frequently throughout part II. This chapter will address three of the most complex and understudied aspects of communication, which involve understanding another person's (1) learning style, (2) generational influences, and (3) leadership/decision-making style, along with the realization that each person views life through his or her own experiential lens.

These three aspects of communication do not occur in isolation. Board/superintendent teams have unique characteristics that make these aspects of communication an ongoing challenge. Open communication is especially challenging when the makeup of this team is based on elections, laws, and staff turnover. Having a purposeful plan in place to bring new members onto the team while bidding departing members farewell can help keep the district on track and moving forward as the turnover and changes take place.

The ever-changing dynamics between and among people are especially relevant when applied to board members and the superintendent. Each election cycle may bring new personalities and interests to the board table and changing superintendents can add complexities that affect the work and progress of the board/superintendent team. To sustain the focus on district priorities, purposeful and continuous relationship building must be fostered.

This partial quotation from Charles H. Spurgeon (1834–1892) sets the tone for welcoming new members to the board/superintendent team: "Begin as you mean to go on, and go on as you began." Intentionally orienting board/superintendent teams with a focus on each other's learning styles, generational influences, and leadership/decision-making styles can build a respectful and productive team. The reward for having a productive team is to maintain a laser-like focus on the most important aspects of the district—improving student achievement and success. The more adults communicate in a civil and efficient manner the more the communication of the district can be on students.

Stepping into professional development designed to address the complexities of board/superintendent interactions and building a working team for the duration that the team is together requires a structured approach. It does not happen by accident. Addressing the variables of learning styles, generational influences, and leadership/decision-making styles using researched approaches can then manifest into a raised level of consciousness about all board/superintendent team members' styles and traits.

Learning Styles. Each board member and superintendent brings his or her own unique learning style to the board table. For example, understanding that some team members prefer a presentation as opposed to reading a narrative report on their own can inform the structure of board and committee meetings. Having a preference for a visual, auditory, or tactile learning style is just one example of learning styles (EducationPlanner.org, 2011).

Generational Traits. The influence of generational traits becomes important with the realization that a board may have members of four generations serving at one time, with a superintendent who is usually a member of one of three generations. Strauss and Howe (2006), who have contributed greatly to the body of literature available on generational differences, advocate understanding the motives of each generation as a way to maintain open communication—both listening and speaking—with an awareness of generational themes.

Leadership/Decision Making. Leadership/decision making requires an understanding of decisions that must be made, deciding who has the authority/responsibility to make decisions, and determining who will be affected by the decisions. Each board member and the superintendent bring unique strengths and personality styles to the board table. These strengths and styles affect how decisions are made. Board members and the superintendent have preferred leadership/decision-making styles and will find themselves using styles dependent upon each situation. Being aware of the array of decision-making and leadership styles among members will assist the board/superintendent team in recognizing and adapting to the variety of styles while doing the important work of the district.

Life Experience. All board members and the superintendent come to the position with rich life experiences. Team members will have their own experiential lens in place during their tenure. Taking the time to learn each other's learning style, generational influence, and leadership/ decision-making style may assist team members as they strive to provide excellent service to the district. Elbert Hubbard, editor, publisher, and writer (1856–1915), stated that "progress comes from the intelligent use of experience." Board members and superintendents have a mandate to move the district forward. By obtaining greater understanding of learning styles, generational influences, and leadership/decision-making styles, boards and superintendents can make progress in addressing the intelligent use of experience.

The three variables explored in this chapter have significant influence over the complex board/superintendent interactions. Each variable and how it can be determined is listed in figure 5.1.

These variables have multiple measurements, which can lead to a determination of an individual's learning style, generational influence, and leadership/decision-making style. Boards and superintendents will want

	Variable	Determination
1.	Learning style	Various assessments. Can include copyrighted assessments. Can include informal self-reports/analysis. Examples: 4MAT, Merrill & Reid
2.	Generations A board serving from 2015-2020 could have members from four different generations	A person's date of birth determines her generation. Four generations - silent (born before 1943), baby boomers (born 1943-1960), gen x (born 1961-1981), and millennial (born after 1981).
3.	Leadership/Decision-making style	Various assessments. Can include copyrighted assessments. Can include informal self-reports-analysis. Examples: Myers-Briggs, Strengths Finder 2.0

Figure 5.1.   Ways to Determine Variables

to delve deeper and perhaps consult an expert to gain further understanding of how to determine each variable.

DETERMINING LEARNING STYLES

Educational psychology research has long reported on whether an individual might be a simultaneous or sequential learner along with a variety of other descriptors for one's learning style. Kolb (1984) has developed a learning style model based on the experiential learning theory. His model utilizes concrete experience, abstract conceptualization, reflective observation, and active experimentation to examine learning styles. There are also quadrant theories on leader/learning styles, which categorize individuals as analytical, driven, amiable, or expressive (Merrill and Reid, 1981).

Indeed, there are various assessments that can measure learning styles. Since the 1980s, Bernice McCarthy has been a leading author and proponent of a method she named 4MAT. This copyrighted approach is based on the theory that there are four basic learning styles that must be assessed and addressed when attempting to understand and improve learning.

While assessments are helpful, individuals can also be asked directly how they best learn. A discussion of learning styles of individuals on the board/superintendent team will encourage appreciation for each other's preferences and may open the door to understanding differences.

GENERATIONAL INFLUENCES

Strauss and Howe (2006; 1991), respected historians and prolific researchers, have advocated for decision makers to gain a better understanding of how generational differences may influence policy makers and administrators (Evert and Van Deuren, 2012). Strauss and Howe stress that educational leaders who understand the motives of a new generation of political leaders are at an advantage. It is likely that board members and superintendents serving from 2015 to 2020 would be a member of one of four generations;

Silent Generation (born 1925–1942)
Baby Boomer Generation (born 1943–1960)

Generation X (born 1961–1981)
Millennial Generation or Generation Y (born 1982–2002)

Figure 5.2 illustrates specific characteristics of individuals who are members of the Silent Generation and Baby Boomer Generation.

CHARACTERISTICS	
Silent Generation **(Born 1925–1942)**	**Baby Boomers** **(Born 1943–1960)**
• Group having fewer children • Quick economic assent • Early marriage, early to have children • Men made educational gains • Higher divorce rate • Increase in helping professions • Strong civil rights leaders • Many bureaucrats • Politically active, challenged rules • No presidents produced	• Result of unusual fecundity and family formation • Received intensive nurturing • Childhood illnesses, diseases • Males have strong ties to mothers • Generation of worsening trends—drunk driving, illegitimate births, suicide • Decline in SAT scores, grade inflation • Sexual revolution more women's than men's movement • Avoiding Vietnam War was more important than serving in military • Believe war was badly handled by GI (WW II) leaders • Left established religions • Supported two pastors for president, Pat Robertson, Jessie Jackson (1988) • Income—men lower than silent generation, women higher

Figure 5.2.   Characteristics of Silent Generation and Baby Boomers (Strauss and Howe, 1991; 2006)

Listed in figures 5.2, 5.3, and 5.4 are characteristics of the various generations. We believe that by studying Strauss and Howe's (1991; 2006) work, certain generalizations regarding the generations can create more in-depth information about how generations can approach the political process.

For example, to capitalize on Generation X's emphasis on accountability, members of the Silent Generation could increase their understanding of accountability laws (NCLB) and measures (standardized tests). Another example of increasing understanding among generations is Generation X board members and superintendents learning about the Baby Boomer Generation's ideology and the Millennial Generation's serious sense of purpose and knowledge of technology.

CHARACTERISTICS	
Generation X **(Born 1961-1981)**	**Millennial/Generation Y** **(Born 1982–1995)**
• Highest abortion rate • Most divorced parents • Most complex families • Domestic (family) dissatisfaction • Believe parents were cool • Grade inflation stopped • Less college than boomers • Prefer military to public service • More conservative • Urban Generation Xers brought weapons to school • More suicides as teens • High incarceration rates • Economic distress has been with them since 1970s • Burden of finances shifted to them—social, retirement • Overcame "cynical Americans" description	• Lowest child-to-parent ratio in U. S. history • Parents want them, low abortion rate • Want quality education • Less poverty than Generation Xers • More Medicaid assistance for youth • Higher savings for youth

Figure 5.3.   Characteristics of Generation X and Generation Y (Strauss and Howe, 2006)

Strauss and Howe (1991; 2006) also report that Generation X board members are more likely to challenge the status quo to a larger degree than Silent Generation or Baby Boomer Generations. The Generation Xers were raised with a *Nation at Risk* (1983) that created doubts about public schools. Thus, GenXers are very protective of their children within the school setting and often see their roles as challenging administrators' decisions. This generational information is helpful for everyone serving as a board member or superintendent.

Strauss and Howe (2006) mention that the Millennial Generation, like the Silent Generation, generally has a higher trust in authority figures, especially compared to Generation X and the Baby Boomer Generation. Millennial employees want to look up to and trust their leaders. Millennials also place strong value on their education and embrace a shift to a new form of economic power: human capital. Human capital includes work ethic and skills (especially technology) and viewing education as an individualized, personalized process. Millennials seek credit for their human capital attributes.

A Special Consideration Regarding Millennials as Employees. Political and employment issues related to Millennials are of particular importance, as Millennials will make up the majority of school employees and a large percentage of political leaders in the next decade. The recruitment of more Millennials may impact hiring practices. For example, Millennials will want to be convinced why they should select a district, as opposed to simply being given a brochure listing wonderful things about their future place of employment.

Millennial recruits frequently consult web sites (75 percent) and may involve parents (25 percent) in the decision-making process (Rebore, 2011). This generation wants their work to be enjoyable and will accept demanding and challenging duties.

Millennials, like previous generations, are interested in fair compensation and will compare their district's benefit and salary package with other districts. Given their strong interest and readiness to keep abreast of their economic status, it may be wise to include them in negotiations, professional development, and other policy development activities. This generation is very politically active and wants a say in the decision-making process.

It is interesting to note that Millennial teachers may consider taking less traditional steps to advance their credentials and train for an administrative position. They are interested, however, in quickly fulfilling training requirements compared to previous generations but do not want their personal lives to become out of balance. Millennials are in a hurry to advance.

Personnel directors, superintendents, and school boards can benefit from learning about Millennial teachers and administrators for placement and induction programs (Rebore, 2011). Millennial employees typically embrace change but within a culture of collaboration, communication, and with minimal isolation and will typically embrace change if they can see its value. Electronic communication is very important to this generation. District leaders face the dilemma of how to find the right balance of electronic and other forms of communicating with Millennials.

Politically, Millennials tend to question news media, businesses, and government. They are cautious in their assessment of whom they can trust. Trust of leaders is a significant consideration for this group. They want their administrators and board members to be transparent, accountable, and model equity in the leadership of a school or school district.

CHARACTERISTICS
Generation Z
(Born 1996–2011)
• Not as large in number as Generation Y/Millennial
• Only know the world with the Internet
• Face a dismal economic picture that will affect how they vote and conduct business
• Attitudes toward frugality may amp up if financial factors do not improve

Figure 5.4. Characteristics of Generation Z (Rebore, 2011)

Generation Z. A fifth generation will soon be on the scene, Generation Z, who will begin roles as board members in the 2020s. They will likely bring a very open attitude and a high level of approval to education, economics, and relationships (Rebore, 2011). The impact of Generation Z will be played out long into the future. It will be interesting for educational historians to understand and record this generation's influence.

LEADERSHIP/DECISION-MAKING STYLE

Boards and superintendents probably have some level of familiarity with learning styles and generational differences. In contrast, they have likely spent less time understanding the variable of leadership/decision-making style. Leadership/decision-making style is a very broad idea that can include basic temperament, strengths and weaknesses, personality traits, and more. Leadership/decision-making styles can be assessed through the use of well-developed, copyrighted, for-purchase surveys, and/or through the analysis of self-reports.

There may be merit to a board and superintendent participating in workshops or study sessions that would include an assessment of leadership/decision-making styles. Van Deuren (2012) has reported 89 percent of board members want professional development with a focus on how board members can better understand district operations, how to improve schools, and the roles of the board and superintendent. While board members and superintendents would be under no obligation to undergo this type of learning experience, doing so could have positive outcomes for students, staff, and the community.

Board members and superintendents must be clear on the potential sensitivity of developing greater understanding of leadership/decision-making styles in a public venue. There are many inventories that can assist with this understanding. One example is the Myers-Briggs instrument, which is based on the personality theory of Swiss psychiatrist Carl Jung (1875–1961) and is predicated on a belief that each individual is born with a predisposition for certain personality preferences (Hoffman, 2002).

The Myers-Briggs emphasizes four areas of personality preferences including the use of senses, intuition, thinking, and feeling. These preferences, combined with whether an individual is more introverted or extraverted and is more or less judgmental, result in sixteen basic patterns of personality that the model ties to a leadership style (Bernes and Nardite, 1999; Hetrick, 1993). Myers-Briggs facilitators are highly qualified to administer the Myers-Briggs instrument and can ensure the reliability and validity of the results.

As the field of psychology has developed, more emphasis has been placed on healthy personalities and individual strengths. One strength-based leadership model is based on the work of former University of Nebraska educator and researcher Donald Clifton (1924–2003). Many school administrators have used the work of Clifton as a basis for interviewing, hiring, and developing talented district faculty, administration, and support staff.

Clifton developed, studied, and implemented his research model and interview approaches nationally during his tenure at the University of Nebraska and through his company Selection Research Associates (SRA). The management consulting company Gallup has since purchased SRA and has promoted the importance of focusing on strengths and talents in education and other fields. The model is explained in the book *Strengths-Based Leadership* by Rath, Clinton, and Conchie (2008). Rath, Clinton, and Conchie stress the importance of an organization studying employee strengths by citing Mervyn Davies, president of Standard Chartered Bank: "If you focus on people's weaknesses, they lose confidence" (p. 54).

Gallup has become a leader in assessing strengths, leadership styles, supervisor-employee relations, and helping individuals increase self-awareness. Thousands of people have taken the StrengthsFinder and it is readily available to boards and administrators. According to Clifton and Gallup's research, there are thirty-four StrengthsFinder themes that naturally cluster into four domains of leadership.

A person's leadership profile is measured through the use of the StrengthsFinder model. Using a forced-choice approach to measure thirty-four strength areas produces results and highlights five talents or strengths. A report is generated that gives an analysis of each of the top five talents or strengths for the individual. *Now Discover Your Strengths* by Buckingham and Clifton (2001) is one method of obtaining a strength profile.

Not all board members will value gaining further understanding of decision-making styles and will continue firm in their judgment that "there should always be a healthy, stressful relationship between the board and superintendent" (Schneider, 2014, p. 12).

COMPLEXITY OF VARIABLES AND THE BOARD/SUPERINTENDENT PARTNERSHIP

Of course, there are other theories of individual growth and development. Boards and superintendents should consider several models before proceeding to use an instrument for professional development. Three variables have been described in this chapter: learning styles, generational influences, and leadership/decision-making styles.

Using a study session or workshop format, the following section provides a model of how boards and superintendents could study, discuss, and analyze how understanding these variables can improve relationships and teamwork. The goal, as always, would be to improve board/board and board/superintendent communications to promote staff and student success through positive policy development and decision making.

A HYPOTHETICAL CASE STUDY OF A BOARD/SUPERINTENDENT WORKSHOP

Context. Our journey into analyzing the three variables begins by establishing the context for our district—let's call it the East Waboo School District. Here are the district's demographics:

- Town population: 35,000
- School district population: 7,000 students, 1,000 employees
- One superintendent of schools: *Millie*. Age fifty-one, fifth year as superintendent

- Board members' age, number of years served, and occupation:

  1. *Bob*
     Age seventy-four, fourteen years of board service
     Occupation: Farmer

  2. *Mary*
     Age sixty-four, eleven years of board service
     Occupation: Bank supervisor

  3. *Sue*
     Age sixty-one, five years of board service
     Occupation: College vice president

  4. *Steve*
     Age fifty, five years of board service
     Occupation: Computer specialist

  5. *Mike*
     Age forty-seven, two years of board service
     Occupation: Owns repair business—self-employed

  6. *Angela*
     Age thirty-five, two years of board service
     Occupation: Works at home, part-time computer software specialist

  7. *Corey*
     Age thirty-one, one year of board service
     Occupation: Surgical nurse

Setting. The board and superintendent interact in an informal and positive manner. Four members of the board were involved in hiring Millie, the superintendent, five years ago. Although the first year of Millie's tenure was stressful, the second and third years were smooth sailing for the board and superintendent. The past two years have been described by the local media as "push and pull," with the board and superintendent having to deal with difficult, entrenched issues including fiscal problems, technology upgrades, problematic teacher negotiations, and declining test scores in math and science.

While the problems are real, there is also a sense of optimism that the district can get better. The board, faculty, staff, and administration seem to be committed to district improvement and there appears to be minimal undercurrents eroding board/superintendent trust.

Action and Cost. In a creative move, the board and superintendent agreed that for improvement to take place, it would be helpful to better understand their own and each other's leaning styles, generational influences, and leadership/decision-making styles. They agreed to use a workshop format focused on general understanding, awareness, and improvement and to not use a "hot-button issue" or "managing crisis" approach as the best avenue for growth.

The board and superintendent agreed to take $10,000 from the superintendent's professional development fund and assess, with a professional facilitator, their learning and decision-making styles. Each board member and the superintendent completed two inventories—one for learning styles and one for decision-making styles—a month prior to the workshop. The results were sent back to them two weeks prior to the workshop by the facilitator, Dr. Agreement.

Board members and the superintendent agreed that all information could be presented and discussed openly at the workshop. The local media did not use the information in a negative manner. Everyone also agreed to share their birth year to determine their generations. All agreed that the results could be made public record and were supportive of the innovative approach to enhance understanding and communication. All participants were willing to explain and justify expenditures for the activity and the importance of enhancing the effectiveness of the board and superintendent. In addition to completing two inventories, board members and the superintendent were asked to provide a written report of how they learn best and want information presented to them in the future.

Grids Showing Complexity of Board Member and Superintendent Variables, Interactions. Dr. Agreement prepared a master list of where the board members and the superintendent were placed on the continuum of learning styles, generation, and leadership/decision-making styles.

The results are found in figures 5.5, 5.6, and 5.7.

Board Members and Superintendent
Placed on continuum depending on the results of the inventory and self-report

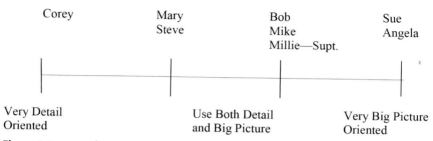

Figure 5.5.   Learning Styles (Clustered according to similar characteristics)

Board Members and Superintendent

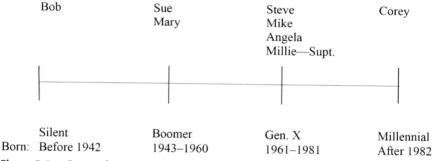

Figure 5.6.   Generations

Board Members and Superintendent
Placed on continuum depending on results of inventory and self-report

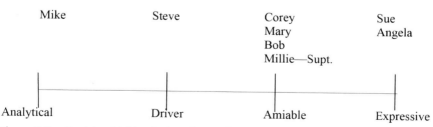

Figure 5.7.   Decision-Making Style (Clustered according to similar characteristics)

The board and superintendent conducted two half-day workshops (September, October) to review their results. The later part of the second day was spent in preparation for a third and final half-day meeting (November). The final meeting was devoted to discussing, listing, and determining how the information could improve relations among the board members and between the board and superintendent in order to improve the district. At the final meeting, all agreed that the process was helpful in the following ways.

RESULTS AND RECOMMENDATIONS FOR IMPROVEMENT

General Results and Recommendations

- The focus on better understanding interactions among board members and the superintendent sent a strong message to the community that all parties were committed to improving the organization. In his 2008 book, *Six Secrets of Change*, Michael Fullan writes about the importance of systemic learning (p. 14). He emphasizes the importance of understanding the complexity of an organization through committing to a system and increasing knowledge. Buckingham and Clifton (2001) stress the importance of organizations focusing on training opportunities that emphasize strengths and investing in ways to improve outcomes. There was strong agreement that the workshop on increasing understanding of learning styles, generational influences, and leadership/decision-making styles was worthwhile in terms of improving the district.
- The process helped further everyone's understanding of each other's backgrounds, experiences, styles, strengths, and talents. There was agreement that this workshop experience could lead to common professional language and to a higher level of trust and communication.
- The process revealed that policy makers and decision makers can benefit from tapping into the strengths of fellow team members. Board members and the superintendent agreed to use this information when assigning memberships to committees and task forces. For example, it may be important to have two or more learning styles on the finance committee to ensure that information is presented in more than one

format and from more than one perspective. The board also decided to have several decision-making styles represented on the building and grounds committee, which has been tasked with studying a possible facilities referendum. They committed to what Gallup's work with leadership teams describes as "while each member has his own unique strengths, the most cohesive teams possessed broader groups of strengths" (Rath, Clinton, and Conchie, 2008, p. 22).

- Through the process of discussing similarities and differences among the board members and between the board and the superintendent, a greater understanding and appreciation of the role technology plays in education and leadership development was cultivated. The group agreed to further study what Smith, Chavez, Seaman, and Barrett (2014) describe as the new era in education—the Conceptual Age. As with any training or professional development opportunity, the need for new fields of study and learning emerged.

Specific Results and Recommendations

- All team members and the media treated the information in a positive, professional manner. There is recognition that it requires courage to publicly reveal personal information. Revealing personal information used in this workshop was not negative or harmful. Board members, the superintendent, citizens, or the media could make this a negative event. There was also acknowledgment and recognition that there are no legal or ethical requirements that any board member or superintendent participates in workshops, nor should there be any recrimination of any individual who chose not to participate.

The costs were acceptable to the board and superintendent. There were two types of costs:

1. *In-kind*

   - Board/superintendent preparation: completing inventories, reading, learning (per board member and superintendent)—five hours
   - Three half-day workshops (per board member and superintendent)—twelve hours

   AND

2. *Actual costs*

- Facilitator: twenty hours of preparation and twelve hours of workshops—total of 32 hours x $100/hour = $3,200.00
- Materials, food, etc. = $1,000.00

Total actual expenditures = $4,200.00
Note: District annual budget = $120,000,000.00
Superintendent Professional Development annual budget = $25,000

SUMMARY

Gaining a better understanding of three seldom-considered variables can enhance board/superintendent interactions: learning style, generational influences, and leadership/decision-making style. We strongly encourage board members and superintendents to give this chapter consideration when determining how to improve team functioning to lead to greater student and staff success. The success of any workshop or study session is the discussion and deepened understanding that carries over from the session. The specific inventories and tools used are less important than the willingness to use a process to interact in a positive, insightful manner.

REFERENCES

Bernes, L. V., and Nardite, D. (1999). *The sixteen personality types: Descriptions for self-discovery.* Hollywood: Radiance House.

Buckingham, M., and Clifton, D. (2001). *Now discover your strengths.* New York: Free Press.

EducationPlanner.org (2011). *What is your learning style?* Retrieved from http://www.educationplanner.org/students/self-assessments/learning-styles.shtml.

Evert, T., and Van Deuren, A. (2012). *Making external experts work.* Lanham, MD: Rowman and Littlefield.

Fullan, M. (2008). *Six secrets of change.* San Francisco: John Wiley and Sons.

Hetrick, W. (1993, March). *Leadership for a time of change.* Paper presented at the Annual Conference on Creating the Quality School, Oklahoma City, OK. Retrieved from http://files.eric.ed.gov/fulltext/ED357933.pdf.

Hoffman, E. (2002). *Psychological testing at work.* New York: McGraw-Hill.

Kolb, D. (1984). *Experiential learning: Experience as the source of learning and development.* Englewood Cliffs, NJ: Prentice-Hall.

McCarthy, B. (1996). 4MAT. Retrieved from www.aboutlearning.com.

Merrill, D., and Reid, R. (1981). *Personal styles & effective performance.* Boca Raton, FL: CRC Press.

Rath, T., Clinton, D., and Conchie, B. (2008). *Strengths-based leadership.* New York: Gallup Press.

Rebore, W. (2011). *Human resources administration in education: A management approach.* Boston: Pearson.

Schneider, P. (2014, May 29). Evaluating Cheatham: 12 Madisonians size up the superintendent's first year on the job. Madison: Wisconsin State Journal, Capital Times Supplement, p. 12.

Smith, S. K., Chavez, A. M., Seaman, G. W., and Barrett, P. L. (2014). *A how to guide for digital convergence in education, blended instructional models, architecting a blended curriculum, digital learning platforms, and one-on-one learning environments.* ModernTeacherPress.com.

Strauss, W., and Howe, N. (1991). *Generations.* New York: Quill.

Strauss, W., and Howe, N. (2006). *Millennials and the pop culture.* Great Falls, VA: Lifecourse Associates.

Van Deuren, A. (2012). *School board member needs and interests regarding the content, structure, and delivery and other considerations related to school board professional development.* Doctoral dissertation. Milwaukee, WI: National Louis University.

6

The Effects of Existing Community Culture on Board/Superintendent Relationships

Bette A. Lang and Pamela Kiefert

Dr. L. K., a new superintendent in a conservative, cash-strapped district, decided it would be a nice gesture to share the refreshments usually reserved for board members with the small audience in attendance at the board meeting. Dr. L. K. was captured on video as she offered snacks and beverages to audience members prior to a board meeting. This video was posted with a voiceover complaining that tax dollars now go to feed audience members at board meetings, stressing that the new superintendent obviously does not understand the poverty level in the district and that all revenue should go to supporting classrooms. How could such good intentions go bad? This scenario is just one example of how a superintendent, not attuned to the local context and not knowing what questions to ask, learned the hard way about the culture of the district and the community.

Culture manifests in a wide variety of ways at every level of an organization and in the community. People keep culture alive. Education is the business of people and helps set the stage and provide the infrastructure for organizational and community culture. According to Deal and Peterson (1999), culture is "an underground flow of feeling and folkways (winding) its way within schools, or the form of vision and values, beliefs and assumptions, rituals and ceremonies, history and stories, and physical symbols" (pp. 7–8).

As much as we know about culture, there is still much work to be done regarding the establishment and functionality of the culture in the board/

superintendent relationship. In his book *The Future of School Board Governance* (2008), Alsbury, citing Burlingame, identifies culture issues in the following manner:

> More research is needed on the "culture clash" that often occurs between superintendents and school boards with long histories of "uniqueness." Every school board in every community has a particular history, a way of doing things, which greatly affects (either positively or negatively) the leadership initiatives of superintendents. The local context plays a major role in superintendent-school board relationships (Burlingame, 1998). (p. 127)

Life as a school board member includes serving as the bridge between the community and the school district. Board membership involves knowing the community's culture, usually by merit of long-term residency, and connecting with the district's culture to provide an optimal learning environment and education for students. Two of the board's primary responsibilities are to hire and evaluate the superintendent and establish goals. An important consideration for boards is whether and to what extent the board goals include a plan to acclimate this new leader to the district and community and to help the new superintendent build on the unique culture in which he or she will work and live.

Superintendents can be appointed or hired from the inside or outside of an organization and community. Past experiences shape their views of education, their role and leadership in a district, and their position and presence in a community. Clarifying a superintendent's past experiences and perceptions and joining them with the new district's and community's culture is challenging for both the board and the superintendent; however, this process is necessary if each board/superintendent team member's uniqueness is to be valued, respected, and useful in building positive board/superintendent relations.

The school board and new superintendent are responsible for melding the local context with the superintendent's past experiences and perceptions. It is important for all team members to recognize that seemingly small details can become large distractions if there are no procedures in place to address them. Newly elected board members may share some of these concerns about local culture, even though they typically have longer residency in their districts.

Questions such as the following have been heard over the years from school board members and superintendents:

- Can audience members partake in the coffee and cookies available at board meetings?
- How should superintendents socialize with board members and the public?
- Which service group should superintendents join?
- Which school district events are implicitly mandated as "command performances" for superintendents and board members?
- Which community events are required for board members and/or superintendents to attend, and which community events should be avoided at all costs?
- How do superintendents gather information and how does a board share the "uniqueness" of its school district in order to avoid a negative impact on the board and superintendent relationship?
- How do superintendents learn the local culture?
- How do boards of education communicate the unique aspects of the district to superintendents and newly elected board members?

Regardless of the responses to the questions above, communication becomes the critical tool for learning and sharing local context. "Communication" as used in this chapter is construed broadly and refers to actions, words, and behaviors that govern interactions, rituals, and habits. Most importantly, this communication is fraught with "hidden rules" that govern it. These hidden rules refer to the unspoken rituals and habits of a group, which may or may not be evident to the casual observer.

Individual districts and communities may define hidden rules in a variety of ways that can range from parking lot etiquette for the superintendent to hiring practices that cater to district graduates, friends, and family. Inquiring about the hidden rules of a district and community requires high-level communication skills that must be used with sensitivity and with reserved judgment because important cultural vulnerabilities may be exposed. These cultural vulnerabilities may reflect very different mores between newly elected board members and/or superintendents' past experiences and present expectations.

Information provided in this chapter is based on current interviews with board members and superintendents on these cultural topics. Four school board members and seven superintendents, with experience in rural, suburban, and urban districts, were interviewed for this chapter. The total number from both groups represents three states and three regions of the country, which enabled us to take a "snapshot" of a variety of cultural and communication issues over a large geographical context.

THE BOARD AND SUPERINTENDENT RELATIONSHIP STARTS WITH HIRING PRACTICES

One board member who shared his perspectives on establishing effective board and superintendent relations stated that the culture of the district should be presented beginning with the posting of the superintendent position. If in-depth knowledge of board governance, individual and group communication techniques and skills, and being present at every district and community function are important to the board, these preferences should be listed in the posting. During the superintendent interview, questions should measure the superintendent's level of experience, knowledge, and ability in these areas, as well as other areas in the job description.

District and board goals should reflect majority interests of the board, the mission and vision of the district, and should also be presented in the job posting and interview questions. Once established, both the superintendent and board should honor the goals or seek open and formal board action to change them. A culture that encourages either the superintendent or board members to work outside the official meeting process on goals that are not approved by the entire board will create an unhealthy governance structure and unproductive board/superintendent relations. Using agreed-upon and open techniques to establish goals and to share and learn the culture of a district can facilitate ongoing positive board/superintendent relations.

Using a search firm to hire a superintendent can help a board present the goals, mission, and vision of the district and the district and community's unique aspects and culture. The search firm acts as an objective outside facilitator that ensures that what is being put forth as important qualities for the next superintendent align with what the board, district, and community want and expect. Superintendent candidates typically lack shared experiences with the board and community, and getting advice and information from board members, human resources departments, or search firms could provide these shared experiences. The rituals, values, and shared experiences can come through during interviews, with superintendents asking questions of the board, such as the following:

- Of what are you most proud in the district and community?
- What do you wish could be changed about the school or the community?

The responses can assist the superintendent with planning to be part of important and high-profile events.

The Description of the Job. Superintendents have a job description. This job description lists the legal requirements for licensing, job responsibilities, expectations, and the ending statement of "everything else not listed above and required by the board of education" or a statement to this effect. One superintendent interviewee suggested that the uniqueness of the district and the local context could be delineated under that final statement in the job description.

School board members have rules and policies that are designed to regulate and guide their behaviors and decisions. Newly elected board members receive these documents and new board members' effectiveness can be directly related to their familiarity, understanding, and implementation of these rules and policies.

Specific, unanticipated, and unwritten job requirements and expectations that involve things like snacks at the board meetings, memberships in service clubs, participation in parades and community events, and where to park in the office parking lot can all create situations that become larger than life in this high-tech world. Negative videos gone viral or reader posts to articles in local newspapers not only distract from the primary function of the district, but may also undermine the credibility and effectiveness of superintendents and board members.

Board and Superintendent Job Expectations Associated with Social Media. New superintendents and board members can benefit from the awareness and use of social media tools. In our research interviews, superintendents and board members mentioned the growth of social media, the impact of social media on their respective positions in the district, and the need to plan the use of these communication tools in order to take advantage of and capitalize on opportunities. In addition, social media must be carefully managed and monitored to avoid problems. In the interviewees' experiences, culture in districts and communities can be communicated effectively using social media tools.

Both superintendents and board members need to consider how negative and erroneous information can be communicated through social media outlets and make handling this type of information part of the culture. For example, one interviewee shared that his district is not engaging in the use of social media due to the conservative culture of the district. Using the district web site and the local newspaper helped his district control the information being distributed by the district and communicated the actions taken in board meetings, leaving little room for errors and rumors.

How can a new superintendent and newly elected board members learn the unique culture of a district? Board members stated in their interviews that they do not think about the culture of the district when hiring a new superintendent, nor do they typically think about orienting a newly elected board of education member regarding cultural issues. Unless current board members are asked specific questions, they reported that they do not provide information on the culture of the district. The interviewees reported that their boards do provide the mission, long-range plan, and other operational documents to candidates for the superintendency and citizens running for the board. They reported that newly elected board members also receive orientation by the superintendent and the board president.

Shared Experiences as an Element of Culture. One of the challenges for new superintendents is that they often do not have shared "local experiences" with the board. In addition, board members, particularly newly elected members, may not have shared local experiences with other board members. Tapping into this important aspect of culture may be an especially difficult journey for externally hired superintendents and board members who are new to the community.

If the whole community should be improved through the work of the board and superintendent, structuring ways to share and learn about the unique culture of the district and community become imperative. Districts could include unique cultural information in new board members' orientation program or instruct the district human resources department or search firm to include unique community cultural aspects with other information being shared with the new board/superintendent team members. This purposeful inclusion of cultural context may provide new board/superintendent team members with a positive foundation for developing shared experiences.

Superintendents who were interviewed shared suggestions for learning about unique cultural aspects of the district and community. Establishing meetings with internal and external stakeholders is a standard procedure for new superintendents. A recommendation was made to interview external groups first and then internal groups second to determine whether the community's perception of its schools was the same as employees' perceptions of the schools. Any disparities found using this method can be useful in establishing a communication plan and superintendent and board goals.

Suggested questions for the internal and external interviews can include asking of what they are most proud, what they would like to see changed, and any surprises the superintendent might expect. The interviews from superintendents serving in both large and small districts revealed interesting cultural tendencies based on district size and, secondarily, the district's level of urbanization.

Our interviewees revealed that responses from community members in smaller districts tended to focus on program offerings (e.g., Advanced Placement classes, co-curricular activities) and on students' work ethic as the means to obtain eligibility for a university or career path. The interviewees' experiences in larger districts appeared to suggest that programs in the district elicited the most pride, with a secondary focus on student commitment. The perception that teachers are less respected and teacher morale was lower was mentioned more often in relation to larger districts from both internal and external stakeholders in those districts.

ESTABLISHING A COMMUNICATION PLAN

A strong board/superintendent communication plan is a critical component of any successful board/superintendent team. Understanding the local context is one of the first steps in establishing a strong communication plan. Superintendents must learn district culture, the thinking behind it, and reactions to decisions of formal and informal groups; that is, they must learn "how and why we do things this way" in order to develop an effective communication plan with their boards. Doing less can produce a misstep that can cause a superintendent and board to experience tension and, at worst, can lead to a parting of ways. Working with the board to establish a communication plan can be mutually beneficial to new superintendents and newly elected board members alike.

Most superintendents new to districts can use the insights gained in the interview process to start establishing the communication plan. One veteran superintendent shared that he presents a list of communication questions during the interview process with the board. Having had the experience of learning about local context through trial and error in past superintendent positions, he now asks key questions about the board's preferred methods of communication, their expectations for socialization with the superintendent, and the community's expectations for the superintendent. The responses to these inquiries can be the basis for a communication plan and a map to bridge a new superintendent's past experiences to the local context of the new district.

Another superintendent shared her transition to a new to a district. As a result of her experience, she now makes asking questions about communication a "must" in order to continue to strengthen the board and superintendent relationship.

This superintendent arrived in her new position armed with good verbal and written communication skills. She drafted a communication plan, which gained board approval. Over the course of her first few months on the job, she kept receiving an invitation to a small local restaurant for breakfast with the citizens and others who gathered every Thursday morning. The invitation was rather brusque and was usually accompanied by "free advice" on how she should be doing her job.

Being wary of special interest groups based on past experience in a larger district, the superintendent politely avoided meeting this group, even though the invitation for breakfast came regularly. Much to the superintendent's chagrin, this breakfast group had the attention of several board members through family ties and longstanding friendships. These board members, after hearing complaints about the superintendent's avoidance techniques, began to lose faith in the superintendent's ability to relate to key stakeholders. The focus of the board began to shift from student achievement to the superintendent's performance and required purposeful interactions and enhanced communication to get the board/superintendent relationship back on track.

How was the superintendent to know that the breakfast group was an influential, informal group? The superintendent's past experiences affected her ability to discern the importance of the group as it related to the board. Should she have mentioned the breakfast invitation to the board president? While it seems in hindsight that a discussion with the board president would have been a good idea, including a question about formal and informal groups with whom the superintendent should meet in the establishment of the communication plan is a prudent move. Such a plan could have helped the superintendent avoid this bump in the road that adversely affected the board/superintendent relationship.

A sound communication plan that establishes a process to set and clarify expectations of both the superintendent and the board can create a pathway for addressing the unique situations a superintendent encounters and the unexpected behaviors the board believes the superintendent is exhibiting. Two communication vehicles include (a) the superintendent evaluation, which may be structured to allow for discussion of unique situations that affect the superintendent's performance, and (b) board meeting agenda planning, which may be tailored to cover specific situations as they arise. Both vehicles create a forum for board/superintendent discussion within legally permissible frameworks.

A third superintendent, new to the position in a small rural district, had been mentored by a superintendent during his tenure in a large suburban district. He had observed the suburban superintendent working with board members and been coached repeatedly to treat all board members equally, work for the majority of the board, not to socialize with board members individually or as a group, and to stay out of the fray. (A veteran superintendent published this same advice in the April 2000 publication of *The School Administrator*.) The new superintendent's mentor encouraged his mentee to communicate and operate with the above advice in mind.

Imagine the new superintendent's surprise the morning following his first board meeting, when three board members came to his office at three different times, all unannounced, and presented their individual agendas. None of the board members brought these specific items to the discussion while the communication plan and goals were being formulated during the board meeting. Each board member had excellent rationale for his or her position. Unfortunately, the agendas of the three board members conflicted with each other's agendas and the recently developed goals and communication plan of the board of education and superintendent.

The new superintendent was taken aback and remained silent. Silence is often interpreted as agreement. His lack of comments and questions led each board member to believe his or her agenda found favor with the superintendent, who, by virtue of his position, would add strength to each board member's agenda.

Remembering his mentor's advice to not step into the fray, he called the board president, explained the situation, and suggested that the three board members have their items placed on a board meeting agenda for discussion. The board president, who had the longest tenure on the board, chose not to follow this suggestion because, in his opinion, these items had come forward before and been voted down. This course of action left unresolved issues between the superintendent and three of seven board members. In the new superintendent's mind, he was never able to establish a sound working relationship with the board and consequently his tenure in this district was short.

IDEAS AND TIPS

Our thanks to the four board members from four Wisconsin school districts and seven superintendents from rural, suburban, and urban districts in three states who participated in interviews for this chapter. They presented many interesting and effective ways to learn about the uniqueness of the district and the local context.

The following are tips and ideas for board members and superintendents who are new to a district and/or community:

1. As a superintendent, understand that you have knowledge of the job, licensure, and background for your new position; however, you do not have the local context. Start out by asking the board, "How do we do things around here?"
2. As a board member, you likely have lived in the district for a long time or have moved into the district and have been a resident for

at least a few years; you must accept that you are steeped in community and district customs and mores much deeper than the new superintendent, especially if he or she comes from another community. Practice empathy and reach back to remember anything you found unique about the community and share that information with the superintendent—even if he or she doesn't ask.

3. As the new superintendent, schedule a meeting to discuss communication planning and ask board members how they prefer to communicate with the superintendent and with each other. Make this information a central and primary focus of the communication plan. Logistics to be addressed include: (a) superintendent's primary contact (usually the board president), (b) the use of email and its distribution (to all board members), (c) written and oral communication as public record, and (d) expectations for socialization (e.g., after board meetings, holiday parties, co-curricular events).

4. If you are a long-time community member and/or board veteran, search your memory bank to remember the unique items and situations past superintendents and newly elected board members experienced or noted. Sharing successes and failures from the past with the new superintendent and board members will be useful to one and all.

5. Depending on the size of the community and district, board members and/or the superintendent may be related to, friends with, and/or business associates or neighbors of district employees. Bring these relationships to each other's attention to avoid conflicts of interest and controversial interactions that can result from dealing with problems and complaints because of not knowing the community and district connections.

6. As a new superintendent or newly elected board member, ask about the "sacred cows" in the district. For example, there are likely certain annual events, traditions, and/or unique programs and courses that seemingly will last forever. If certain items are not on the budget reduction list or certain courses are always run irrespective of the enrollment, mention this information to new board members and the superintendent.

7. As a new superintendent, minimize the use of acronyms and jargon so as not to alienate the board, staff, and community.

8. Be vigilant about "walking one's talk." Superintendents and board members who espouse specific beliefs and then act or vote opposite to that belief undermine their credibility and the stability of the district. These actions also contribute to an unhealthy culture. Examples include: (a) board members publicly stating that community input is vital and then setting policy to limit public comments at board meetings to one minute and (b) a superintendent stating that teamwork is valued and then continuously sending out top-down decisions for administrators to implement. These types of behaviors lend themselves to an unhealthy working environment.

9. A key "keeper of the history" of the district and community can be the administrative assistant to the superintendent. The administrative assistant is usually an individual hired from the community. If this person has been in the position for a reasonable length of time, he or she knows the culture of the district and community, the items and situations that past superintendents and newly elected board members may have struggled with, and the wide variety of relationships, connections, and associations that exist within the district and community. New superintendents and board members will be well served to ask the administrative assistant for coaching and advice.

10. If a search firm is being used to hire the new superintendent, candidates should ask the search firm about the district and community's unique aspects, culture, and vulnerabilities. If the board or the human resources department is facilitating the hiring process, the same inquiries should be made.

There is a saying that if a person attends to the little things, the big things take care of themselves. In education, both little and big things matter; however, when learning a district and community culture, it is usually the little things that get overlooked and not shared that distract from the district's primary purpose. To address this concern: ask questions. Ask lots of questions. And share, share, share with new board members and superintendents!

QUESTIONS FOR REFLECTION AND DISCUSSION

- How does a superintendent learn the governance structure of the board?
- How does he or she anticipate the unresolved issues that might become insurmountable and shorten his or her tenure in a district?
- How can he or she discuss the board members' relationships with each other?
- How can a board know how the new superintendent will react to unresolved issues?
- How does a board discern the superintendent's ability to deal with competing board member interests?
- What kinds of structured, specific hiring techniques and interview questions can be pivotal in addressing these concerns?

REFERENCES

Alsbury, T. L. (2008). *The future of school board governance.* Lanham, MD: Rowman and Littlefield Education.

Deal, T. E., and Peterson, K. (1999). *Reframing the path to school leadership.* Thousand Oaks, CA: Corwin Press.

Eleven Tips for Savvy Superintendents—the Communication factor in superintendent success. (2008). *National School Public Relations Association.* http://www.nspra.org/files/docs/SavvySuperintendents.pdf.

Fuqua, A. B. (2000, April). A board divine or divided: Sustaining a positive relationship. *The School Administrator.* https://www.aasa.org/SchoolAdministratorArticle.aspx?id=14126.

Kolb, D. (1984). *Experiential learning: Experience as the source of learning and development.* Englewood Cliffs, NJ: Prentice-Hall.

7

Unanticipated Departures of Superintendents

Thomas F. Evert and Amy E. Van Deuren

The superintendency is far from a stable position within the school district. The average tenure of the superintendent is 3.5 years (Black, 2009). This fact is such common knowledge that there is an adage among superintendents that they should keep their suitcases packed under the desk. Every superintendent position carries with it an inherent risk that the acting superintendent will not stay in the position until the end of the contracted term.

Why do superintendents leave and how does the process work? This chapter will address those questions by focusing on two aspects of unanticipated departures: (a) characteristics of departures during certain stages of a superintendent's career and (b) what to expect during the unanticipated departure process.

Departures occurring at various stages of a superintendent's career will be discussed using the Superintendent Experience Framework (Evert and Van Deuren, 2013). This framework identifies certain tendencies for unanticipated departures shared by individuals with similar years of experience in the superintendent role. The departure process will be discussed using a framework adapted from the world of emergency preparedness, an Unanticipated Departure Framework (Evert and Van Deuren, 2013). Each framework provides a way to think about and think through issues around unanticipated superintendent departures that should be considered by every practicing and aspiring superintendent.

Both frameworks were developed as part of research in which twenty-two school superintendents who experienced unanticipated departures were interviewed in depth. Each was given the freedom to tell his or her own story in his or her own way, guided by key questions to ensure every superintendent covered the same topic areas during the interview. These interviews enabled us to recognize emerging patterns and to develop some conceptual frameworks that might help superintendents navigate a departure process in a way that minimizes potential damage to his or her career, the school board, and, most importantly, the district.

SUPERINTENDENT EXPERIENCE FRAMEWORK

The data collected for the study of unanticipated superintendent departures revealed that the commonalities of experiences seemed to have a relatively strong connection to the number of years an individual had served as a district leader. Simply stated, superintendents serving in their positions for three years or less tended to undergo unanticipated departures for reasons related to their inexperience, while those superintendents with four to nine years of experience and more than ten years of experience tended to have different reasons for their departures.

Interestingly, the superintendents interviewed for this project were distributed relatively evenly across the three experience groups. Seven superintendents experienced an unanticipated departure after less than three years' experience, six superintendents experienced unanticipated departures between experience years four and nine, and nine superintendents experienced unanticipated departures after ten years or more of service as a superintendent in the same district. While each departure was unique in many ways, the common characteristics found in each of the three age range groups are described below.

Less Than Three Years' Experience. Many of these superintendents indicated that they chose positions that were not a good fit. Some recognized this lack of fit from the start and took the position anyway. They did so for understandable reasons: it is an interesting paradox that it is commonly believed that a shortage of school superintendents exists, yet it is still a difficult position to obtain. This reality leaves many first-time superintendents in positions that they may recognize as a poor initial fit, but they often try to make the best of less-than-ideal positions in the interest of beginning this leadership phase of their careers.

This group also tended to encounter board member resistance early—very challenging board resistance that would likely test the skill of any superintendent regardless of experience level. The "honeymoon period" between the board and superintendent was very brief, if it even existed at all. These new superintendents were unprepared for the level and type of board resistance that they faced almost from the first day on the job. This regular and ongoing resistance manifested itself in many ways, but the combination of inexperience and pressure took its toll and resulted in an unanticipated departure before the end of the contract period.

Another important characteristic that this group shared was a steep learning curve in achieving a manageable work/life balance. The responsibilities and learning curve of the superintendency in the first years are such that finding time for any personal endeavors or time with family and friends can be very challenging. The superintendents who left during their first years on the job acknowledged that they became entirely absorbed in the work, allowing no time for any other personal enrichment. Over time, this lack of balance had a negative effect on their work.

Finally, these inexperienced superintendents were more likely to accumulate "rocks in their pockets," which are the negative accumulations of the political capital spent making many small and large decisions over time. That is, these superintendents made a series of decisions that were not cost effective in terms of political capital and, over time, their effectiveness was diminished as their influence over stakeholders was eroded. Eventually, their influence erodes so much that they have none left to engage in effective leadership and leaving is the only option.

Four to Nine Years' Experience. This group was in many ways the most diverse in experience and the most interesting. They had survived many "trials by fire" early in their superintendent careers, felt stable in their positions, and understood their value to the district they served and to the profession in general. Over 50 percent of respondents felt that they had choices; that is, they were not "railroaded" into an unanticipated departure by the board. They had established overall functional board/superintendent relationships for the most part and had also established a functional work/life balance.

The reasons for the departures in this group were varied, with the most interesting characteristic being that many of the superintendents initiated the departure themselves for one of two reasons. First, the superintendent recognized that a situation had arisen that was untenable and that it would damage the district less if the superintendent left than if he or she stayed. Second, the superintendent applied for or was sought after for another position and decided to make a career move before the end of his or her contract.

The superintendents in this group, although not personally unaffected by the departure process, seemed to possess the greatest inherent resiliency, willingness to move on, and most objective perspective regarding their positions and careers.

Ten or More Years' Experience. This group of superintendents had, as a whole, enjoyed many successful years of service as a superintendent, with positive board relations and an impressive list of accomplishments in their district or districts of service. These superintendents tended to experience unanticipated departures as a result of shifts in the board. Sometimes these shifts were subtle and happened over time, and sometimes they happened suddenly over the course of one election cycle.

For those superintendents who experienced subtle shifts in board personnel over time, there eventually came a point at which none of the original board members present at the time of hire were still serving on the board. These superintendents noticed over time that support for superintendent-backed programs and initiatives was eroding. The most direct evidence of eroding support was a shift in votes, noting that, one vote at a time, board members went from supporting the superintendent on most initiatives to opposing him or her. It eventually became clear that the opposition was not about the initiatives but about the superintendent.

For those superintendents who experienced a dramatic shift over one election cycle, the unanticipated departure was often particularly unpleasant. In these instances, a shift in one or two board members instantly changed the entire dynamic of the board from one that worked in collaboration and cooperation with the superintendent to one that was clearly and fully in opposition to him or her. In these situations, it was often clear that the new board members wanted new leadership. These unanticipated departures often took place relatively quickly (often a year or less) and were extremely difficult on the district and on the superintendent.

LEADERSHIP LESSONS

What do these commonalities among superintendents with varying experience levels tell us? Most importantly, they tell us that no one in the superintendency is immune to an unanticipated departure. Second, your experience (or lack thereof) can work against you in different ways, depending on whether you are starting out in your career or at the end of your career. Third, as the group of superintendents with four to nine years of experience indicates, the superintendent/board relationship is one of balance and if either side does not like the balance, they can make choices to remedy the situation—so you have choices, regardless of how difficult a departure situation may seem.

These leadership lessons segue very well into the next framework that will be reviewed: the unanticipated departure framework. This framework views an unanticipated departure from the superintendency as a process, not as a singular event. Much like a boater takes safety precautions when venturing out on the water, with safety gear in tow in case of an emergency, a savvy leader takes safety precautions when entering into a leadership position and has gear ready in case an emergency should arise that places him or her in a position of a possible unanticipated departure.

UNANTICIPATED DEPARTURE FRAMEWORK

The idea for the Unanticipated Departure Framework was modified from the National Incident Management System (NIMS) used by the Department of Education (DOE) in crisis management. The NIMS crisis management model consists of four phases: (a) preparedness, (b) prevention and mitigation, (c) response, and (d) recovery (http://www.rem4ed.com/terms/terms.html). The Unanticipated Departure Framework also consists of four (slightly different) phases: (a) preparation, (b) recognition, (c) management, (d) recovery and reflection.

Each of these four phases covers a part of the process that a superintendent undergoes during an unanticipated departure. Some of the suggestions in these four phases can (and arguably should) be considered by anyone serving or aspiring to be a superintendent as a safety precaution, while other pieces of the framework need only be implemented at the time when a crisis is at hand.

Preparation. One of the worst ways to prepare for an unanticipated departure is to think it will never happen to you. It could. Taking a position as a superintendent includes an inherent risk that you will have to leave your position quickly and unexpectedly—more so than in any other public school position. Realizing that it *could* happen to you is the first step in being prepared in case it *does* happen to you.

Based on the superintendents interviewed, the most important way to prepare for an unanticipated departure is actually a preventative measure, and often the hardest one (especially for a new superintendent) to do: be sure that you feel in your heart and mind that the position you are being offered is a good fit for your values, skills, experience, and dispositions.

The bottom line is that if you're getting a sinking feeling in your gut or some other communication from your mind and body that tells you something is not right, trust it! Probe deeper with the board and district personnel either to quell that "gut feeling" or to give you additional evidence that your instincts are correct. This suggestion is much easier said than done, especially when loans loom, families must be supported, and careers are ready to be launched.

The next important preparation step has to with managing your finances, especially regarding big purchases like a home. Often, boards are anxious to have new superintendents become part of the community, and many see a home purchase as an important part of belonging. There are plenty of superintendents who end up carrying two (or even more!) mortgages as they change jobs and the homes that they purchased do not sell. Consider purchasing a home with ease of resale in mind, so that if you face an unanticipated departure, more options for moving forward with your life and career can be considered.

The third important preparation step involves family and loved ones. The decision to pursue a career as a superintendent carries a higher-than-normal risk of an unanticipated departure, after which chances are very good that a move to another town or city will be necessary. Making these career decisions with a family fully aware of the risks, the visibility (in good times and in bad times), and the ever-present possibility of relocation will make the unanticipated departure process, should it occur, much more bearable for everyone close to the superintendent.

Two other important points merit mention in this preparation phase. First, budget personal funds for an attorney so that the funds are available should you need one. A departure transition can affect your financial stability, so budgeting for legal expenses can greatly mitigate stress during a departure process. Second, keep an open mind regarding your career and career moves. With high-level district administrative positions, it is sound advice not to get too attached to any one job or place because research clearly shows that these jobs have an extremely high turnover rate.

Recognition. Recognition is that critical moment when a superintendent realizes that an unanticipated departure is imminent. Whether it happens suddenly or gradually over time, whether it is initiated by the board, the superintendent, or from another constituency, everything changes after that realization. The paradigm shifts from one in which the superintendent is the leader and is responsible for problem solving in the district to one in which the superintendent's leaving *is* the solution to the problems in the district.

The threshold question for most superintendents when faced with a situation likely to result in an unanticipated departure is whether to fight or leave. It is not uncommon for superintendents to seek the counsel of family, friends, clergy, legal counsel, and even psychologists. During this process, the superintendents we interviewed talked at length about the need to remain as objective as possible, monitor health and personal habits, and keep emotions in check and under control. They worked hard to get the most realistic assessment possible about the full extent of their situation so that they could make intelligent choices.

Many signs can point to the realization that an unanticipated departure may be in the future if a person takes the time to assess them. Assess personal health, especially any effects of prolonged periods of stress that can provide solid information about whether a departure is a good move. Assess district climate toward leadership, working relationships, and relationships with stakeholders to notice any recent changes. Reassess your own perceptions to determine whether you are seeing things as they are or whether you need help from someone with a more objective lens. Look at the political role of the superintendent and the agendas of others in relationship to that role. Assess key decisions and small decisions along the way.

Opening lines of communication with the board during this recognition phase can also be valuable in determining whether a departure situ-

ation exists or whether issues can be resolved. These lines of communication will be necessary whether the situation is resolved or whether it
moves toward an unanticipated departure. Trying to maintain the status
quo after the realization that the problems or issues might result in a
change in leadership does a disservice to the superintendent, the board,
and/or the district.

Of critical importance is managing personal emotions during this time.
Many of the superintendents interviewed cautioned against "the road of
despair." The departure process is a time when a leader needs to be at his
or her best in order to make the best decisions for the district and for a
personal career moving forward. It is highly recommended to assemble a
"team" of support when the recognition phase occurs, including family,
friends, trusted colleagues (not in the district), church connections, and/or
trained professionals to help you as you work through the next phases of
the departure process.

The recognition phase is typically very short, but it represents a critical
juncture at which a person moves from leading a district to managing a
departure. Priorities and objectives shift dramatically and a different set of
leadership skills are required to make the best of a less-than-ideal situation.

Management. At this phase of the unanticipated departure process,
the departure is imminent. There is no longer any question about fixing
problems; now the focus is on negotiating a departure agreeable to all parties. If that sounds like "legalese" that is because a departure before the
fulfillment of a contract requires a legal separation. Many superintendents
(although not all) hire an attorney to help them work through the terms
of the separation and early termination of the contract. Being represented
by an attorney can ensure that the departing superintendent is receiving a
complete, legal, and equitable severance agreement. For example, many
negotiated agreements in unanticipated departures include "nondisparage-
ment" clauses that require that neither side speak ill of the other side.

No two unanticipated departures are alike in their timelines, terms, conditions, and settlements. Sometimes, the board is able to meet with the superintendent to discuss departure terms; other times, the relationship is so
eroded that the superintendent meets with the board through an attorney.
Factors that affect departure terms, timelines, and conditions include the
length of time left on the contract, whether the superintendent has another
position lined up, or whether the board has a new leader in mind.

The management phase of the departure cycle requires that the departing superintendent manage his or her own emotions and conduct to ensure that long-term damage to the district is mitigated as much as possible. The management phase of departure can bring with it a large amount of ugliness in terms of media attention, heightened scrutiny and unwanted attention from internal audiences and external publics, and relentless pressure from the board. When superintendents discussed this aspect of the departure, many expressed how difficult it was, but stressed their commitment to do the job they were hired to do: lead and protect the district to the best of their ability.

Those superintendents who were able to stay "district focused" (and thus "student focused") made better decisions for the health of their districts and, ultimately, for themselves. Nothing was to be gained by acting unprofessionally or out of negative self-serving interest (such as revenge), and much was at stake in terms of the district and community and their ability to move forward from this stage to reestablish order and control and continue to work toward positive student and staff results.

Managing an unanticipated departure has a tendency to take a toll on the physical health and well-being of the departing superintendent. Many reported that they experienced new health issues or that existing health issues became worse. Some respondents reported succumbing to common stress reactions, like overeating or drinking too much. Other respondents indicated that they were very careful about their health and made a conscious effort to avoid these stress reactions so that they would have the stamina and mental clarity to make good decisions for their districts and for themselves.

Supporting and being supported by family, friends, spiritual leaders, and/or mental/physical health professionals during the management phase is critical to a successful departure. This phase is arguably the most difficult for family and friends of the departing superintendent, especially if the departure is receiving significant media attention. Most superintendents acknowledged that the experience brought them closer to family and friends, although many also acknowledged that professional acquaintances that they considered friends quickly distanced themselves once the unanticipated departure became public knowledge.

The management phase of an unanticipated departure process is often the most challenging and most public. This phase will typically challenge the superintendent's physical, mental, and emotional stamina to their limits. A support system of family, friends, and professionals can help the superintendent work through this process and leave the district and themselves as whole as possible. Despite the fact that the superintendent is undergoing an unanticipated departure, the superintendent is still the district leader until the moment he or she is not. All of the details of the departure must be managed within the context of continued leadership.

Recovery. As with most of life's defining moments, there is life afterward. Recovering from an unanticipated departure takes time, whether it is weeks, months, or years. The process is hard physically, mentally, and emotionally on the departing superintendent, the family of the superintendent, and many district employees who work closely with the superintendent. Thoughtful reflection and taking time to absorb the lessons learned has helped many superintendents better understand what happened and come to terms with their role in why the departure occurred and how it played out.

Once an unanticipated departure has occurred, the overwhelming advice was to get out of the district and community. Above all, superintendents advised avoiding the temptation to follow the district in the news, follow blogs, or engage in gossip with former colleagues. Such activity is ultimately a losing proposition no matter how you look at it. You will feel bad because the district is getting along fine without you, or you will feel bad/guilty that the district is not doing well and it is your fault. If the district is not doing well and you do not feel guilty about it, then that says something else about your future capacity for leadership.

Many superintendents experiencing unanticipated departures had new positions arranged before they left the departure district. Most superintendents advised that if you plan to continue service in a leadership position to get that new position as soon as possible. However, some suggested that taking some time for reflection and healing before moving to that next position was critical for a successful recovery. Regardless of whether you wait or move to the next position right away, the chances are very good that the new position will be a better fit for your skills, strengths, and interests.

Maintaining strong support systems after the departure occurs is important to ensure a healthy healing process. In any leadership position, having an effective support system in place is a critical tool for success in good times and in tough times. Cultivating relationships that ensure your personal well-being is as important to your leadership effectiveness as cultivating relationships to promote your district's well-being.

SUMMARY

Unanticipated superintendent departures occur with enough regularity that they are known and accepted risks of the superintendency; yet formal planning and training for such departures are not a part of most super-intendents' preparation portfolios. Knowing the common reasons that superintendents experience unanticipated departures and understanding that an unanticipated departure is a process, not a single event, can help current and future superintendents begin to create a plan in the event that they should find themselves in an unanticipated departure situation.

No superintendent is immune to the risk of unanticipated departure. The highest levels of skill, knowledge, and competency do not protect an individual from the possibility of such a departure occurring. Simply put, no job protection exists in the superintendency. While there are often underlying issues related to the "fit" between a superintendent and dis-trict (especially for less experienced superintendents), an unanticipated departure is often driven by a complex interaction of forces outside the superintendent's locus of control. The best way to avoid the most unpleas-ant effects of an anticipated departure is to acknowledge and identify the potential risk and create a plan that will help you recognize and work through the departure process should it occur.

REFERENCES

Black, S. (2009). The interim CEO. *American School Board Journal, 196*(4), 53–54.

Evert, T., and Van Deuren, A. (2013). *Thriving as a superintendent: How to recognize and survive an unanticipated departure.* Lanham, MD: Rowman and Littlefield Education and American Association of School Administrators.

III

HIRING ISSUES

8

Board Considerations for Hiring Superintendents

Bette A. Lang and Joel A. VerDuin

From policy making to politics, school districts are under amplified pressure to increase student achievement. Superintendents are expected to be instructional leaders who lead school districts toward high performance. The metrics that define performance are often in the form of test scores, achievement gaps, and/or graduation rates. In any definition of performance, student achievement is the new benchmark for identifying how well a school is doing and how well a leader is leading. It is not surprising that superintendent turnover rates remain high and school boards are all too frequently in the position of having to choose a new district administrator.

Hiring the superintendent is often seen as one of the most critically important aspects of board governance. The importance of this task is reinforced by literature from the National School Boards Association (2006) and a study of Wisconsin school boards (Rindo, 2010). While there is some agreement in literature about the definition of the "right" leadership attributes and skills, the ways school board members define the right set of attributes and skills in a new leader is not as well known.

This chapter examines effective leadership qualities and school board hiring processes. The author used a meta-analysis provided by Marzano and Waters (2009) and the characteristics defined in their work as a lens to examine how five school districts conducted their hiring processes and where in the processes identification and definition of desirable leadership abilities and traits were evidenced.

While hiring processes for the superintendency vary to some degree, most boards use a profile of the traits the successful candidate will possess, use interview questions, participate in deliberations, and conduct reference checks to fill this leadership position. Superintendents who participate in the hiring process often wonder what happens when the board closes the door and meets in closed session to select the new superintendent for the district. Much has been written about the qualities a board wants in a superintendent; however, little has been written about which characteristics a board actually considers.

In their analysis of district leadership and traits that affect student achievement, Marzano and Waters (2009) cite five specific leadership behaviors that positively correlate in a significant manner with increased student achievement. This positive correlation confirmed the link between district leadership and student achievement across the schools in a district. The five specific leadership behaviors are:

1. Ensure collaborative goal setting.
2. Establish nonnegotiable goals for achievement and instruction.
3. Create board alignment with and support of district goals.
4. Monitor achievement and instruction goals.
5. Allocate resources to support goals for achievement and instruction.
   (p. 6)

The key to successful superintendent and board leadership, which can and does influence student achievement, is to strike a balance between providing principals with sufficient autonomy coupled with clear district-wide structuring and monitoring of goals. Superintendent and board leadership is key to attaining this balance to positively influence student achievement. To what level do boards consider these five specific leadership traits when they hire superintendents?

METHOD AND DATA COLLECTION

The author surveyed school boards in five school districts with student populations ranging from 1,500 to 10,000 students. Three of the five districts used a search consultant to lead the selection process and two districts developed their own superintendent hiring process. Each district provided a detailed description of their specific hiring process.

RESULTS

All five boards provided superintendent candidates with profile questions used in the initial screening of candidates. All five boards provided the researcher with the formal, written questions asked during the closed session interview. Three of the five boards provided the researcher with questions asked during the reference check process. Interestingly, none of the boards responded to researcher requests to provide narrative information on how the deliberations to determine the next superintendent progressed. As a result, we will continue to wonder about what actually occurs during these high-stakes deliberations.

Interview Questions. The interview questions were analyzed and revealed that several questions related to the five leadership behaviors were incorporated into the boards' interview process. The following list shows the combined districts' use of questions corresponding to the five leadership behaviors:

1. Collaborative goal setting: ten questions
2. Goals for instruction: thirteen questions
3. Board alignment: three questions
4. Monitoring progress: fourteen questions
5. Allocating resources: four questions

The sample of districts for this study was small; however, it is worth noting that consultant-led (three districts) versus non-consultant-led (two districts) superintendent interview processes differed in the total number of questions used. Both consultant-led and non-consultant-led results indicated board alignment and allocating resources were the two leadership behaviors receiving the least board attention.

The number of questions varied between districts with the number of total questions ranging from sixteen to seventy-eight. The largest district used a total of sixteen questions in a consultant-led search. A mid-size suburban district used the most questions (seventy-eight) and did not use a consultant for their superintendent hiring process. In addition, the large district used one round of interview questions, while the mid-size suburban district used three rounds. The use of a consultant in the large district may have affected the number of rounds of interviews. In general, these data reflected the varied nature of superintendent hiring processes.

With student achievement as the goal of every school district and Marzano and Waters's research defining the five leadership behaviors of superintendents that lead to the highest level of surveyed instruction and achievement, using interview questions that determine the presence of these five behaviors could help ensure a sound process producing a successful hire.

Through VerDuin's process of coding, categorizing, and counting data to present the presence of these leadership behaviors, the tables in this chapter were established and represent the interview questions that best matched each leadership behavior. What follows are descriptions of each of the five leadership behaviors and identification of indicators coded to match the definition of the behavior.

Collaborative goal setting refers to the superintendent's desire to jointly establish district goals with various constituent groups. Table 8.1 displays the various statements and questions board members made to match the collaborative goal-setting theme.

Across all school districts and all four stages of hiring processes, a total of ten questions or statements matched the concept of collaborative goal setting as shown in table 8.1.

Nonnegotiable goals for instruction and achievement are described as being goals that address two specific areas. First, the superintendent who demonstrates these leadership qualities develops and communicates, and second, the superintendent who expects improvement in the areas of instruction and student achievement. Table 8.2 displays the statements related to this leadership behavior.

Table 8.2 displays the number of indicators that describe leadership behaviors focused on improving instruction and student achievement. These thirteen indicators represented all school districts and all four stages of the hiring processes.

The third leadership behavior is the alignment of the school board to support district goals. This behavior is demonstrated when school boards have a clear focus on the nonnegotiable goals for instruction and achieve-

Table 8.1.   **Collaborative Goal-Setting Indicators**

Number	Statements/Questions
1	A successful public school system has a clear and focused direction that is consistently maintained. Who do you believe has the primary responsibility for establishing that direction?
2	The individual we wish to hire for this position must have the desire to encourage innovation and creativity and the ability to focus students, staff, and community on the educational goals of the district.
3	Visionary leader able to craft, communicate, implement, and realize the goals of his or her vision for the district.
4	The goal of continuous improvement across all areas of the school district's operations is expected based upon goals jointly developed with the school board.
5	Describe how you encourage creative thinking and motivate staff to garner ownership in district goals and initiatives.
6	Describe how you prefer to set goals for the school district.
7	Welcomes the opportunity to frame a new strategic plan to guide the district's initiatives for the next several years.
8	Develop a shared vision of a preferred future with board members and stakeholders and clearly articulate the vision to staff, parents, and the community.
9	Someone with an inclusive management style that can inspire disparate groups to define common goals and work together to achieve them is strongly desired.
10	How would you determine long-range and short-range goals for the district? Whom would you involve in the planning process? What would you consider as the "strategic" component of such a plan? Have you had experience building such a plan and what stakeholders were involved?

ment and little else rises to an issue of priority. Table 8.3 displays the questions or statements related to the behavior of board alignment.

Table 8.3 displays indicators that match the concept of aligning the school board to nonnegotiable goals for instruction or achievement. Of the five leadership behaviors, board alignment of goals had the smallest number (three) of questions or statements found in the data in all five districts.

Monitoring achievement and instructional goals is the fourth leadership behavior. The concept of monitoring achievement involves the use of data or assessments to determine success toward nonnegotiable goals for instruction and achievement. Additionally, statements or questions

Table 8.2. Nonnegotiable Goals for Instruction and Achievement Indicators

Number	Statements/Questions
1	Provide leadership in developing and maintaining the best educational programs and services.
2	Develop educational goals for the district with appropriate timelines and action plans for accomplishment.
3	What is the superintendent's role in curriculum development?
4	How would you go about instituting curriculum change?
5	How would you handle opposition to curriculum change?
6	What have you done to improve educational accountability/student achievement in positions you have held? What improvement indicators, beyond test scores, are important?
7	Increased focus on closing the achievement gap between white, middle-class students and their peers of different backgrounds.
8	Data-driven and research-based decisions made with an "ear to the ground," listening to all constituents.
9	Exhibits a desire to hold staff accountable for continuous improvement.
10	What is the role of the superintendent in the development and implementation of the district's curriculum?
11	Describe programs you have implemented to improve instruction and student achievement.
12	Share a curriculum goal that you and your staff recently accomplished.
13	He or she should have a laser-like focus on student learning and building a strong instructional program.

Table 8.3. Board Alignment and Support of District Goals Indicators

Number	Statements/Questions
1	Report quarterly and annually to the board and the district on goal-achievement progress.
2	How would you assist the board in identifying its roles and responsibilities in relationship to governance and the operation of the school district?
3	Describe the school board's role in strategic planning and how you would assist with planning efforts.

that demonstrate a process of accountability were considered a match to this leadership behavior. Table 8.4 includes all indicators found within the data that match the concept of monitoring progress toward goals of instruction and achievement.

Table 8.4. Monitoring Goals for Instruction and Achievement Indicators

Number	Statements/Questions
1	Develop and maintain a system of evaluating the adequacy of the educational program; assess problems and areas of weakness; develop monitors to evaluate the problems; plan for resolution; take corrective action; and evaluate the change.
2	Describe how you would ensure continuous improvement is taking place in all programs offered by the school district? Provide examples of the tools you use to analyze student progress and report results to the school board.
3	How would you evaluate the need for, or impact of, curriculum change?
4	Describe the indicators you would use to determine success or excellence in the district.
5	Describe what role you would play in the assessment, monitoring, and delivery of instruction in the district.
6	How do you/would you use assessment results in making judgment/ decisions regarding a school's effectiveness?
7	How do you/would you monitor that school administrators use assessment results to make instructional decisions?
8	How do you use student assessment to improve instruction?
9	What have you done to improve educational accountability/student achievement in positions you have held? What improvement indicators, beyond test scores, are important?
10	Demonstrates a keen understanding of student assessment and how it can be used to foster high academic achievement.
11	What is the role of the superintendent in the development and implementation of the district's curriculum?
12	Give us a short example of how you have helped the district's teaching staff and administration use data to improve instruction and test scores.
13	Explain how you would monitor the implementation of the district's strategic plan.
14	How would you implement short- and long-range district goals? How would you monitor and evaluate their implementation?

All five districts' results indicated monitoring goals for achievement and instruction as having the highest number of indicators (fourteen) when compared to the other leadership behaviors. In these examples, comments that indicated the use of data or assessments are considered matches to the concept of monitoring progress. In addition, matches were considered when statements or questions addressed issues of monitoring the progress of strategic plans.

The fifth leadership behavior is the allocation of resources toward nonnegotiable goals for instruction and achievement. In the documentation submitted, many questions and statements were presented regarding the topic of budgeting. However, a large number of indicators addressed managing a budget or strategies for budget reductions. Table 8.5 lists the concepts that matched the allocation of resources leadership behavior.

Table 8.5. Allocation of Resources to Goals Indicators

Number	Statements/Questions
1	Given limited resources, how would you propose to adequately balance resources between the instructional needs of the district and deferred maintenance needs?
2	What priority do you give core academic curriculum and instruction? What about arts and athletic programs?
3	How do you identify budget priorities in an era of tight finances? What level of oversight do you expect from the school board?
4	In your current position, how have you planned ahead with the current and future economic difficulties facing education, and what steps are you specifically taking to safeguard student learning?

Table 8.5 displays statements and questions regarding the allocation of resources to support instruction and achievement. Data that did not include specific statements about instruction or student learning did not qualify as matching the concept of allocating resources for the improvement of instruction or achievement. There were four responses from a total of three districts.

Along with the leadership behaviors presented by Marzano and Waters, VerDuin found two additional behaviors that school boards desired based on the hiring process questions used. The two skills were communication and relationship building. Table 8.6 lists statements and

Table 8.6. Strong Communicator

Number	Statements/Questions
1	Communicate changes in board policies to employees and explain their effects.
2	Inform and advise the board about the programs, practices, and problems of the schools, keeping the board informed through quarterly reports with recommendations for improvement.
3	Establish and maintain a program of community relations to keep the community well informed of the activities, needs, and successes of the school district, effecting a wholesome and cooperative working relationship between the community and the schools.
4	Describe how you communicate with staff, community, and the school board in ways that provide clear and concise messages. Provide examples of specific communications techniques.
5	What methods have you found to be most effective when communicating with staff, community, and board?
6	What are some ways you communicate with your immediate staff, administrators, teaching, and support staff?
7	Many people in the community feel disconnected with the school district. What are some methods you would use to increase contact with the community and promote the district?
8	Possession of good communication skills.
9	Give examples of the kinds of information you deem important to provide to the school board, when, and via what method.
10	List several methods of communication you consider most important.
11	How does he or she share information with staff in his or her position?
12	Increased and improved communication from board to staff.
13	They desire an experienced, communicative leader with a strong, engaging, inclusive personality.
14	Visible in the schools and in the community.
15	Excellent communicator.
16	Exceptional communicator to all stakeholders in the community.
17	How do you build relationships with the community in which you work?
18	The ideal candidate will possess strong communication skills and demonstrate his or her abilities in previous positions to interact in positive ways with staff, students, parents, and community.

(*continued*)

Table 8.6. *Continued*

Number	Statements/Questions
19	It is expected that the superintendent will reside within the school district and be highly visible in the community.
20	Maintains open and honest two-way communications with all persons based on good listening skills and a willingness to consider divergent points of view before reacting to or deciding upon issues of importance to the school district.
21	Describe your preferred communication style and provide examples of how you have inspired trust and positive working relationships with school personnel and community.
22	How do you prefer to communicate with the school board outside of board meetings?
23	How do you ensure that all segments of the school community receive information and how do you encourage questions and feedback from those not directly in the schools?
24	Describe how you would introduce yourself to staff and the greater community.
25	What do you do to improve public relations and to foster good communications among the students, staff, parents, community, and school board?
26	Personal characteristics high on everyone's list are excellent communication skills.
27	Excellent communication skills.
28	Give a few specific examples of how you make yourself visible within the community and how you have successfully communicated with citizens, staff, and board members about your district's problems and accomplishments.

questions used to determine a candidate's skill level in communication and relationship building.

Strong communication skills appeared with a high degree of frequency ($N = 28$) in the data sets provided by school district officials and shown in table 8.6.

Table 8.6 displays the number and variations of statements and questions related to the superintendent exhibiting strong communication skills. Interestingly, the significant number of statements and questions is substantially higher than any of the five leadership behaviors identified in the data.

The second skill area was as a relationship builder. The data contained many statements with varied wording about the concept of the superintendent as a builder of relationships both internally and externally. Table 8.7 displays the varying statements and questions identified as matching the concept of relationship building.

The sixteen responses from five districts described in table 8.7 include any statement or question related to building relationships with people internally or with community members. It is significant to note the total number of relationship-building indicators shown in table 8.7 was also higher than any of the other five leadership behaviors qualified in this study. Communication statements were very similar, but to qualify for relations building, the statement or question needed to indicate some purpose for communications, such as building trust.

VerDuin's dissertation research on this topic produced the following results based on five districts reporting, with three of the five using a consultant to assist in hiring. His finding was that the use of a consultant had a minimal impact on the presence or absence of indicators related to the five leadership behaviors. His research also indicated that some of the leadership behaviors were more prevalent than others, with the most prevalent being establishing goals for achievement and instruction and monitoring these goals.

VerDuin also found that the skills of communication and relationship building were highly sought through the stages of recruitment and interviewing in the superintendent hiring process. These skills were identified in the literature as being important skills for superintendents to possess, as reported by school boards and embedded in the Interstate School Leaders Licensure Consortium (ISLLC) Standards.

Every hire made in a school district is important. Boards of education make one direct hire and that employee is responsible for accomplishing the work of the district. Thus, the use of focused, purposeful hiring practices that produce a superintendent candidate who will process the five leadership behaviors found to improve student achievement and instruction should be required practice. In addition to five leadership skills, boards must also focus on communication and relationship-building skills.

Table 8.7. Relationship Building

Number	Statements/Questions
1	Establish and maintain a program of community relations to keep the community well informed of the activities, needs, and successes of the school district, effecting a wholesome and cooperative working relationship between the community and the schools.
2	Collaborate with community programs and groups in meeting the diverse needs of students within and beyond the school environment.
3	Describe the specific role in the community as you see it.
4	Part of a successful school district hinges on relationships between local government, community groups, and other community members. Please share with us an example of an initiative you have led that was successful in improving these relationships.
5	A person who values and secures community engagement by establishing relationships between schools, local government, and business institutions.
6	Passion for strong community relationships.
7	What methods do you employ to ensure your visibility with staff, students, and the community?
8	How involved is he or she in the community?
9	Describe your preferred communication style and provide examples of how you have inspired trust and positive working relationships with school personnel and community.
10	The district is composed of a number of small communities and covers a wide geographic area. How would you schedule your time to ensure that staff and the public have opportunities to interact with you throughout the course of the school year?
11	Describe your level of community involvement. Provide examples of a special project or initiative you have been involved with at the community level.
12	Personal characteristics high on everyone's list are excellent communication skills and outstanding interpersonal relationship skills.
13	Strong team-building skills that produce collaborative relationships between and among administrators, teachers, support staff, board members, and community.
14	Visible in schools and community, interacting comfortably with students, staff, parents, and community members.
15	Team builder.
16	Tell us about the specific strategies or methods you use to build and maintain a collaborative working relationship with the teacher's union. What worked best for you and what did not work well?

REFERENCES

Council for Chief State School Officers. (1996). *Interstate school leaders licensure consortium: Standards for school leaders.* Washington, D.C.: Author.

Marzano, R. J., and Waters, T. (2009). *District leadership that works: Striking the right balance.* Bloomington, IN: Solution Tree Press.

National School Boards Association. (2006). *Becoming a better board member: A guide to effective school board service.* Arlington, VA: Author.

Rindo, R. J. (2010). *High impact district governance: Effective school board member actions and practices.* Doctoral dissertation. Madison, WI: Edgewood College.

VerDuin, J. (2011). *The relationship of leadership qualities to Wisconsin school superintendent hiring practices.* Doctoral dissertation. Madison, WI: Edgewood College.

9

Hiring Internal Candidates for Superintendent

Annette Van Hook Thompson and Linda K. Barrows

Hiring the right superintendent for a school district is one of the most important decisions a board will make. When the fit or match between superintendent and board works, the critically important work of school boards and superintendents can flourish. One would think that understanding the factors that influence this hiring decision would be well researched; however, little research exists that specifically addresses hiring internal candidates for leadership positions.

Superintendent candidates fall into two basic categories. They are either internal candidates (individuals previously or currently employed by the school district) or external candidates (individuals who have never been employed by the school district). Distinct differences exist between internal and external candidates, as is the rationale employed by the school boards in selecting these individuals. This difference exists primarily because of the level of prior knowledge that the board has regarding the candidates.

In this chapter we will discuss recent research conducted to learn more about the factors that influence school boards to hire an internal candidate as their superintendent. We will focus on three consistent themes that emerged from the research. First, we found that personal characteristics, especially integrity and trustworthiness, were of paramount importance to school board members involved in the decision to hire an internal candidate for the superintendency. Second, we found that when hiring internally, school board members were seeking change agents rather than individuals who would maintain the status quo of the organization. Third, the credibility of the hiring process was found to be particularly important for the superintendent who was hired from within.

Based on the results of this research, implications for school board members and aspiring superintendents will be discussed. School board members will want to know the extent to which personal characteristics influenced hiring decisions, the extent to which the desire for a change agent was a factor in the hiring decision, and the importance of board dynamics in the hiring process. Aspiring superintendents should be familiar with the advantages and disadvantages of being promoted from within and the importance of establishing a trusting working relationship with school board members in order to advance the district's success.

BACKGROUND ON THE ISSUE OF
HIRING INTERNAL CANDIDATES

For several reasons, the process of selecting the right person to serve as superintendent has become increasingly more difficult for school boards. First, the candidate pool is dwindling as Keane and Moore (2001) concluded from their research, which analyzed the reasons behind a shortage of applications for Michigan superintendencies. The National School Boards Association (NSBA) also noted this trend of fewer applicants. The NSBA states that "search consultants report that vacancies in some major school districts draw fewer applicants than used to be the case, and that not all the candidates are well suited to that particular superintendency" (2006, p. 135). In other words, not only is there a shortage of applicants, but the applicants' lack of qualifications is also cause for concern.

Turnover in the superintendent position is another challenge boards face. Although variability exists in the statistics regarding the length of superintendent tenure, current studies show that turnover in this key position occurs far more frequently than is ideal for optimal school governance (Marzano and Waters, 2009). It may seem to a board that they have just concluded a search for their superintendent when it is necessary to begin another search due to lack of longevity in this position.

Related to this frequent turnover data, the *2010 Decennial Study* reported that "only 50.7% of the respondents intend to be superintendents in

2015. The finding foretells a substantial number of career exits in the next 5 years" (Kowalski, McCord, Peterson, Young, and Ellerson, 2011, p. 22). This phenomenon is particularly problematic because recent research (Marzano and Waters, 2009) has confirmed that superintendent leadership has a direct positive correlation on student achievement and that superintendent longevity contributes to that success. "The implications regarding hiring and retaining superintendents are clear. School boards and the local community should seek to provide an environment for superintendents that will make them want to spend a decade or more in one school district" (Marzano and Waters, 2009, p. 114).

Interestingly, although there is a substantial body of research pertaining to superintendents' perceptions regarding the factors a school board considers in making a hiring decision (Glass, Björk, and Brunner, 2000; Glass and Franceschini, 2007; Kowalski et al., 2011), very little has been documented regarding the factors a school board considers for this important decision. "As with many facets of a superintendent's professional life, there is little research assessing how, when, and why school boards hire and fire their district leaders" (Matthews, Floyd, Ilg, and Rohn, 2002, p. 16). Likewise, Kowalski writes, "Unfortunately, only a limited number of studies have examined the reasons why school boards select superintendents" (2006, p. 365).

With fewer individuals applying for superintendent positions, a lack of qualified applicants, frequent turnover of individuals in this key job, and the possibility of a large number of superintendent career exits in the very near future, this hiring decision will become even more challenging for school boards. Given these concerns, a school board may want to consider an internal candidate as the superintendent. Hiring internal candidates is not a new occurrence, but appears to be a growing trend. In a survey of 424 Wisconsin school districts, it was determined that between the years of 2001 and 2009, one out of every four superintendents hired was an internal candidate. In the following two years (2010–2011), the number of internal candidates being hired as superintendents has increased to one out of every three (Thompson, 2012, pp. 81–84). However, the research regarding a school board's decision to hire such an individual is limited.

There are several factors influencing the school board throughout the superintendent hiring decision. Such factors include:

- The school board's hiring practices. *Does the board utilize consultants and/or district constituents in the search process?*
- The school board's desired role of the superintendent. *Is the board interested in an individual who will communicate effectively or a business manager who will efficiently oversee the district's resources?*
- The candidate pool. *Will the board consider nontraditional candidates for their next superintendent?*
- Personal characteristics of the applicants, such as gender, ethnicity, age, experience, or licensure. *How will a board collectively determine the personal characteristics desired in their next superintendent?*
- State of the district. *Will the board select a succeeding superintendent who will maintain the status quo or be an agent of change for the district, and what influence does the exiting superintendent have on the board's hiring decision?*

Hiring practices, personal characteristics, and the overall state of the district emerged from the research as the most important factors influencing a board's decision to hire an internal candidate as superintendent. A detailed explanation of these three factors follows.

INTERNAL SUPERINTENDENT HIRING FACTORS

Hiring Practices. Given the importance of the superintendent hiring decision, school boards generally give a great deal of time and attention to this process. The standard superintendent hiring process begins with a plan to recruit superintendent applicants by developing a position profile and reviewing/revising the job description. Input from key stakeholders is often part of this process.

The second phase of the hiring process is the actual recruitment of applicants. Some boards elect to use a consulting firm while other boards work independently of such assistance. Research revealed that school boards most frequently acted independently from consultants, especially if the district was small. "The increased use of search consultants was associated with district enrollment; that is, the larger a school system, the more likely the board was to retain a search consultant" (Kowalski et al., 2011, p. 73).

During the third phase in the hiring process, applications are screened based on established criteria as articulated in the position profile and job description. At this point, a measure of evaluation enters into the selection process. Selection committee members and/or the consultants assess an applicant's qualifications based on the resume, licensure, educational experience, and recommendation letters.

The fourth phase is the interview process. Generally, the interview questions are designed to elicit responses from the applicants regarding leadership skills, previous experiences, and qualifications in the areas expected for the job. Although typically objective in nature, the interview process often invites subjectivity to enter into the thinking of board members. Board members, consciously or not, may make inferences about an applicant based on appearance, verbal and nonverbal communication, and mannerisms (Matthews et al., 2002). These factors may influence the board's hiring decision.

Following the first round of interviews, finalists are usually selected and asked back for a more in-depth interview that often includes a tour of the facilities and/or the community. In addition, board members may choose to visit the applicant's school and/or community to get a better sense of the leadership that they have brought to their previous position. Finally, the new superintendent is chosen, an administrative contract is offered and accepted, and the new superintendent is announced and becomes oriented to the board and the position.

Personal Characteristics. Making a final hiring determination is frequently highly influenced by a number of subjective factors. The NSBA (2006) states that "the artistry in superintendent selection lies in realizing that objective criteria will provide a list of qualified candidates, but a final choice is likely to be based on individual and collective opinions of how well suited a candidate is to the needs of the community" (p. 137). Thus, an elusive factor of fit or match can and often is the determining variable in the hiring decision.

Examining superintendent hiring trends based on gender, age, ethnicity, and experience can be done with objectivity. Analyzing a hiring decision based on subjective characteristics is complicated and challenging because the chemistry among the superintendent, the school board, and the staff is unique in each district. However, this relationship requires scrutiny because it can determine the superintendent's longevity and his or her ability to bring about change (Kowalski et al., 2011). Nearly half of the respondents (49.2 percent) in the *2007 Mid-Decade Study* reported that leadership ability was the primary reason their current school board hired them as superintendent. "Personality characteristics such as honesty, integrity, ethics, and dedication" (Glass and Franceschini, 2007, p. 68) were the second most common reason given for the decision of the school board to hire the superintendent.

State of the District. The dynamic relationship between the board and the departing superintendent, the formal and informal assessment of the outgoing superintendent's job performance, the morale of the staff, the impressions of the community, and the overall state of affairs can all influence the board's decision in hiring the next superintendent. Likewise, events occurring in the district prior to the hiring decision are likely to affect the board's decision. Such events may include an interest in maintaining progress on initiatives or, conversely, an event that resulted in a loss of trust in the administration (Kowalski et al., 2011).

Balancing a drive to bring innovation and change to a district while at the same time acknowledging and maintaining select elements of programming and personnel can result in either friction between a school board and the superintendent or a determination to work collaboratively. In other words, boards are seeking leaders with skills to either transform a district or sustain established reform efforts (Keane and Moore, 2001). Oftentimes, school boards are looking for a "miracle worker" (Matthews et al., 2002, p. 1), and the tendency is to believe that someone outside of the organization is more likely to possess the skills necessary to change the organization rather than someone already in place.

RESEARCH DESIGN

Employing a sequential mixed-methods research design, a study was conducted to determine to what extent the five factors identified in the literature were present in the decision to hire an internal candidate to the superintendency in Wisconsin in the last ten years. These five factors were identified as (a) hiring practices (Kowalski et al., 2011; Matthews et al., 2002), (b) the desired role of the superintendent (Glass, Björk, and Brunner, 2000; Glass and Franceschini, 2007; Kowalski et al., 2011), (c) the candidate pool (Matthews et al., 2002), (d) personal characteristics (Glass, Björk, and Brunner, 2000; Glass and Franceschini, 2007; Kowalski et al., 2011), and (e) the state of the district (Matthews et al., 2002). Information gleaned from relevant literature guided the development of questions that were used to probe the impact of each of these factors on the hiring process.

An initial survey was sent to all 424 Wisconsin public school districts. Based on the responses of 326 school districts, 86.81 percent hired at least one superintendent between 2001 and 2011. Of those superintendents hired between 2001 and 2011, approximately 25 percent were internal candidates.

A second follow-up survey was then sent to school board members in the districts that hired an internal candidate. A total of forty-two surveys were sent to school board members identified in the initial survey as individuals integrally involved in the decision to hire an internal candidate to the superintendency. Of these forty-two surveys, thirteen individuals responded, which represents a 30.95 percent return rate. School board members who responded to the second survey were asked to explain why the school board decided to hire an internal rather than an external candidate.

Following the survey of school board members, a total of five interviews were conducted. Two interviews were with superintendent search consultants and three interviews were with school board members who participated in their school board's decision to hire an internal candidate as superintendent. The three school board members interviewed served districts ranging in enrollment from five hundred to four thousand students.

WHAT THE SURVEYS AND INTERVIEWS TELL US ABOUT HIRING INTERNAL CANDIDATES

Personality Characteristics: How did personality characteristics impact the hiring decision? Personality characteristics emerged as one of the most important factors in the decision to hire an internal candidate to the superintendency. School board members repeatedly described the desirable attributes of the internally hired superintendent. Common characteristics cited by nearly every school board member who provided responses to the survey and the interviews were honesty, integrity, respect, transparency, and trustworthiness. While the overwhelming emphasis on personality characteristics was expected, it is concerning that attributes such as trustworthiness and integrity—or, more pointedly, the perceived lack thereof—would emerge as such a primary factor in the hiring decision. The link between personality characteristics and a crisis of confidence in the exiting superintendent may account for some of the heightened attention given to this factor.

Superintendent as Change Agent: What effect did the board's interest in preserving or modifying the state of the district have on the decision to hire an internal candidate? A finding emerged that significantly deviated from the expected outcome. The literature suggested that school boards would be more likely to hire an internal candidate when it was their intent to maintain the status quo of the district and would hire an external candidate when they wanted significant change to occur (Kowalski et al., 2011). Repeatedly, respondents discussed their expectation for the internal candidate to bring significant change to the organization. School board members espoused the idea that change would occur, and occur more quickly, due to the internally hired superintendent's knowledge of what needed to be done to have the organization experience progress.

Board Dynamics: What effect did board dynamics have on the hiring process? The relationships among school board members as well as their relationship to the superintendent suggested that school board dynamics were an important factor in hiring an internal candidate (Thompson, 2012). It was evident from the comments made by the superintendent search consultants that getting school board members to agree on the process of a superintendent search was an initial hurdle to overcome, followed by building consensus for the ultimate hiring decision. Several school board members reported dysfunctional board dynamics, which resulted in a limited capacity to focus on the genuine work in which a school board should be engaged. Perhaps diminished productivity of the board is an explanation for why very little emphasis was placed on succession planning or cultivating leadership development within the organization in these districts. Succession planning was expected to be a major factor in the decision to hire an internal candidate.

IMPLICATIONS FOR SCHOOL BOARDS

Board Dynamics. Superintendents' relationships with the school boards, particularly with the boards' leadership, reflect the health of school organizations. Sound, solid relationships between school board presidents and superintendents serve as a model of collaboration to districts seeking to extend the tenure of their superintendent and, even more importantly, to serve as exemplars of educational transformation (Thompson, 2012). When the board functions in a manner that effectively serves the students, staff, and community, then personal agendas, power struggles, and micromanagement are minimized. Trust is reciprocal: if boards expect exemplary conduct from superintendents, then behaving in a like manner themselves is necessary.

Clarity of purpose as it relates to the key work of school boards and mission-focused decisions can help the board develop dynamics that result in a positive, proactive, and productive board. While the superintendent provides the framework for board activities, it is ultimately the school board members themselves who need to monitor and, if necessary, reframe their relationships with each other and the superintendent. As these activities relate to superintendent hiring decisions, it would be helpful for school board members to carefully consider how their actions enhance or sabotage the opportunity of success for their new superintendent—whether that individual was an internal or external candidate.

Succession Planning. Succession planning often involves the deliberate efforts of the organization to develop and promote leadership within the organization. A problem with many organizations, including school districts, is that the focus is on one charismatic individual. However, charismatic leaders often do not stay in the organization very long for a variety of reasons, resulting in a regular turnover in the primary leadership position. In such systems, initiatives are typically unique to the leader's goals and gifts, so such turnover creates problems as each new leader brings new initiatives and methods.

In stark contrast to this system are organizations that focus their efforts on developing leadership within their organization, as Fullan (2008) states in the following:

> Because many leaders are working together, they are constantly cultivating leaders within their ranks for the future. Younger leaders are being groomed for the future of the organization, and when leaders develop other leaders in this way the likelihood of continuity and good direction is greatly enhanced. (p. 111)

In other words, to ensure the continuity of ongoing school improvement, great leaders need to develop and leave behind other great leaders.

Perhaps the most well-known research on the impact of leadership on an organization is Jim Collins's influential book, *Good to Great* (2001). Collins concludes:

> The evidence does not support the idea that you need an outside leader to come in and shake up the place to go from good to great. In fact, going for a high-profile outside change agent is *negatively correlated* with a sustained transformation from good to great. (p. 31; italics in original)

Based on the companies studied in his research, Collins stated that ten out of the eleven "good to great" companies promoted their leadership from within the organization. In an analogy pertinent to educators, Collins uses the image of a school bus: "The main point is to *first* get the right people on the bus (and the wrong people off the bus) *before* you figure out where to drive it" (2001, p. 44; italics in original).

Ultimately, school boards need to be visionaries about superintendent leadership. Planning for the succession of new leadership requires diligence and attention. Leaders are revealed by the opportunities afforded to them. Uncovering this talent within their own organization would be mutually beneficial to all. Therefore, boards and administrators should provide opportunities for current employees with developmentally appropriate opportunities for leadership, including instructional improvement efforts.

Integrity of the Hiring Process. Board members should be mindful of the hiring process, especially when considering an internal candidate. They should employ all steps in the process including development of the job profile, reviewing/revising the job description, recruitment of applicants, application screening, and conducting interviews and community visits before making the final selection. Failure to engage in a comprehensive hiring process may undermine the success of newly appointed superintendents.

In the words of one search consultant, "There's [*sic*] some real disadvantages to the candidate if it's just an internal promotion. People think that the person undersold themselves [*sic*] for the position or salary; they made some kind of deal with the board of education" (Thompson, 2012, p. 100). Boards would be well advised to conduct a credible search process so that the individual selected as superintendent obtains the position on merit rather than perceived convenience or favor.

IMPLICATIONS FOR ASPIRING SUPERINTENDENTS

Relationships. A fitting adage that sums up the experience of being hired as an internal candidate is as follows: "For an inside candidate the good news is the board already knows you. The bad news is the board already knows you" (Matthews et al., 2002, p. 4). Clearly, there are advantages and disadvantages to hiring an internal candidate as superintendent. The NSBA (2006) advises its members:

> Hiring from within the district will provide a superintendent who is familiar with the system, who knows the staff and probably gets on well with any number of teachers and administrators, and who will be a walking advertisement for your board's fairness in rewarding good work. Some boards have found, however, that hiring from within can lead to such problems as stagnation in the district's progress, complacency in the superintendent's office, and a beehive of internal politics. (p. 137)

Internally promoted superintendents are part of the staff and community and as such would need to reframe, at least in part, their relationships with colleagues and community members. Personnel matters could become entangled given the individual's history within the district and could pose challenges to moving initiatives forward. Newly selected superintendents need to consider past relationships as they develop new ones as superintendent.

Agent of Change Expectation. The assumption that the internally hired superintendent does not have his or her own learning curve is a fallacy. Several school board members believed that the internal candidate already knew the needs of the district; therefore, they could make changes exponentially faster than an externally hired superintendent. However, effective leaders know when change needs to occur and how to make that change take place. Change may cause difficulties, and "district leadership must be willing to traverse the turbulent and sometimes treacherous waters" (Marzano and Waters, 2009, p. 108) to bring about the change necessary for an organization to improve.

Compounding the potential for trouble in the midst of change is the fact that sustainable change takes time and therefore, as previously reported, extended superintendent tenure is paramount. We agree with Marzano and Waters (2009) that a reasonable concern for an individual being considered as the new superintendent in a district in which change is being sought is whether or not the school board support will remain steadfast during complex and contentious periods of change as opposed to whether or not the new superintendent is an internal or external candidate.

Importance of Integrity and Trust. Aspiring superintendents need to be keenly aware that the relationship with the school board is paramount to their success in the superintendency. This awareness does not imply that the superintendent is solely responsible for the success of this relationship; in fact, there are dysfunctional school boards that would challenge the skill of any highly effective administrator. Entering the superintendency with a willingness to understand how the school board functions, the ability to build consensus, and the capability to make decisions and interact collaboratively are prerequisites for success.

Effective communication, a focus on building relationships, and a stellar character are the foundational requirements for a healthy relationship with the school board, the staff, and the community. As such, it is critically important for the aspiring superintendent to understand that success in the superintendency and trust are inextricably intertwined. "Trust resembles a fine piece of crystal. It is hard to create, very valuable, and quite fragile" (Badaracco, 2002, p. 27).

Broken trust between the superintendent and the school board is not easily repaired and will likely reduce the tenure of the superintendent. Trust is given in some measure when the school board makes the decision to hire an individual as their superintendent. Likewise, the newly hired superintendent trusts that members of the school board will behave with integrity. This new relationship will require nurturing and affirmation if the vitally important work of providing a quality education to every child in the system is to occur.

It is suggested that current superintendents remain mindful of the ways in which they are perceived by their school boards. Continually displaying steadfast character, transparent communication, and competence in dealing with difficult situations will build the confidence and trust that the school board has in their superintendent.

The personal characteristics of integrity, trustworthiness, and honesty are vitally important to practicing superintendents, especially during turbulent times. Guiding a district requires tenacity, fortitude, focus, and affirmation of others. These characteristics are evident in practicing superintendents through ongoing, effective communication. When complacency settles into a practicing superintendent's attitude, others—including the school board—will likely notice and express dissatisfaction with the superintendent's performance.

Board members and superintendents should consider the following:

- The importance of trust and integrity is paramount in the board/superintendent relationship. The fit or match between boards and superintendents is subjective to a degree and includes the board's attempts to assess leadership abilities by assessing personal characteristics.
- While many may believe hiring an internal candidate will promote the status quo, the opposite may actually be true. Boards may hire an internal candidate to accelerate the change process in a district.
- Board dynamics, as measured on a continuum of functional to dysfunctional, are a critical component to consider when hiring a superintendent, whether an internal or an external candidate.
- Boards are strongly encouraged to discuss and consider a succession planning process.
- Boards must ensure the integrity of the hiring process; that is, a comprehensive and credible search is critical.
- There are specific factors that influence a board during the selection process of a superintendent: desired role of the superintendent, candidate pool, overall state of the district, and more.

REFERENCES

Badaracco, J. (2002). *Leading quietly.* Boston: Harvard Business School Press.

Collins, J. (2001). *Good to great.* New York: Harper Collins Publishers.

Fullan, M. (2008). *The six secrets for change: What the best leaders do to help their organizations survive and thrive.* San Francisco: Jossey-Bass.

Glass, T. E., Björk, L., and Brunner, C. C. (2000). The study of the American superintendency, 2000: A look at the superintendent of education in the new millennium. Arlington, VA: American Association of School Administrators.

Glass, T. E., and Franceschini, L. A. (2007). *The state of the American school superintendency: A mid-decade study.* Lanham, MD: Rowman and Littlefield Education.

Keane, W. G., and Moore, D. (2001). The disappearing superintendent applicant: The invitation to apply goes unanswered. In C. C. Brunner and L. Björk (Eds.), *The new superintendency: Advances in research and theories of school management and educational policy* (Vol. 6). Kidlington, Oxford, UK: Elsevier Science Ltd.

Kowalski, T. J. (2006). *The school superintendent: Theory, practice, and cases* (2nd ed.). Thousand Oaks, CA: SAGE Publications.

Kowalski, T. J., McCord, R. S., Peterson, G. J., Young, I. P., and Ellerson, N. (2011). *The American school superintendent: 2010 decennial study.* Lanham, MD: Rowman and Littlefield.

Marzano, R. J., and Waters, T. (2009). *District leadership that works: Striking the right balance.* Bloomington, IN: Solution Tree Press.

Matthews, J., Floyd, D. G., Ilg, T., and Rohn, C. A. (2002). Succession: Insiders vs. outsiders. *School Administrator, 59*(5). Retrieved from http://0proquest.umi.com.oscar.edgewood.edu/.

National School Boards Association (NSBA). (2006). *Becoming a better board member: A guide to effective school service.* Alexandria, VA: Author.

Thompson, A. (2012). *Factors that influence a Wisconsin school board's decision to hire an internal candidate to the superintendency.* Doctoral dissertation. Madison, WI: Edgewood College.

10

Hiring Interim Superintendents

Jon R. Vollendorf and Thomas F. Evert

School districts are occasionally faced with the challenge of hiring an interim superintendent when it is not the best option to hire a permanent superintendent. This hiring challenge is also faced in businesses and churches. If a school district, business, hospital, or church views the tenure of the interim leader in a positive manner, the time can be very productive and an opportunity to reflect upon the purpose and future of the organization (Dye, Fairley, and Otto, 2008).

School boards and districts have consistently acknowledged the importance of preparing for new superintendent leadership (Johnson and Douglas, 1990). A smooth transition of leadership can be a critical factor in determining district success (Cook, 2006). There is a long history of districts employing various individuals on a temporary basis in leadership positions, including principals, interim superintendents, directors, and others (Sanacore, 1997). Black (2009) stressed the importance of the board/superintendent relationship, which can be extended to the critical nature of superintendent/board interactions.

This chapter is a research report focused on perceptions of expectations school board members had for interim superintendents serving in the last ten years. Additionally, the interim superintendents serving the participating boards were also studied to obtain their perceptions of the expectations that boards placed upon them. This research is focused primarily on the board because they define, write, and measure interim superintendent job expectations that supersede other stakeholders due to legal requirements and authority. This chapter also includes the perceptions of individuals who recently served as interims so that a balanced picture of the interim superintendency is presented.

Surveys and interview questions were used to ask boards and interim superintendents about the expectations and services of interim superintendents in their districts. This approach provided both quantitative and qualitative data for the overall analyses.

RESEARCH PARTICIPANTS:
BOARD MEMBERS AND SUPERINTENDENTS

The participants in the research came from a wide range of district types, with student enrollments between 225 and 10,000 students, with a mean student enrollment of 3,200 students. Ten districts were included in the study; six of the districts were classified as rural and four were classified as urban districts. Most participants in the study had significant experience, either on the board or in the superintendency, and most were members of the Baby Boomer Generation or older (born between 1943 and 1960).

The research also included ten interim superintendents. Nine were male and one was female, and each had served as an interim in the last ten years. Seven of the participants were members of the Baby Boomer Generation (born between 1943 and 1960) and three were members of the Silent Generation (born between 1925 and 1942). The average total tenure of each superintendent was fifteen years as a permanent superintendent, and eight of the ten participants had retired and come out of retirement to serve as an interim superintendent.

Ten board of education members participated in this study. Each board was asked to select one board member who was most deeply involved in the interim hiring process. In cases in which the person most closely involved no longer served on the board, past board members were contacted to participate. Most of the board participants were either current or past board presidents. Of the ten board members, six were males and four were females, two of whom were Generation X members (born between 1961 and 1981). Eight participants were members of the Baby Boomer Generation (born between 1943 and 1960). The average years of board service for the board participants was nine years.

FRAMEWORK AND SURVEY RESULTS

The American Association of School Administrators (AASA) conducted nine major "state of the profession" studies of districts and superintendents from 1920 to the present. The most recent study was conducted by Kowalski, McCord, Peterson, Young, and Ellerson in 2010 with results published by Rowman and Littlefield. Kowalski et al. (2010) has asserted that superintendents must successfully address five major roles, including:

- Instructional Leader: *Focus on teacher development.*
- Business Manager: *Focus on long-range planning, financial and human resources development.*
- Political Statesman: *Focus on community leadership and advocating for public education.*
- Applied Social Scientist: *Focus on the ability to solve problems for a district through use of both theory and data.*
- Effective Communicator: *Focus on collaboration, relationships, and other aspects to build understanding of and support for public education.* (p. 6)

Survey Results. A key board member and the interim superintendent, who worked together in a school district, were asked to rate the perceived role importance and the actual role success of the interim superintendent in the five areas of instructional leadership (instructional leader, business manager, political statesman, applied social scientist, and effective communicator). Survey items were presented using a five-point Likert scale, with five being the highest rating and one being the lowest rating. Results revealed (a) board members' perceptions of role importance and perceived superintendent success and (b) interim superintendents' own perceptions of role importance and their own perceived success.

Table 10.1 illustrates the perceived role importance and the perceived role success as indicated by board members.

Table 10.1. Interim Superintendent Ratings: Board of Education (N = 10)

	Perceived Role Importance	Perceived Role Success
Instructional Leader	3.2	3.6
Business Manager	3.8	4.4
Political Statesman	4.0	4.4
Applied Social Scientist	3.2	3.8
Effective Communicator	4.4	4.2
TOTAL MEAN	**3.72**	**4.1**

Board members perceived effective communication and political statesmanship as the most important roles for an interim superintendent ($M = 4.4$;
$M = 4.0$), followed closely by business management ($M = 3.8$). The least
important roles as perceived by board members for interim superintendents
were that of instructional leader and applied social scientist (both with $M
= 3.2$). It would appear that perhaps the weighting of role importance is
affected by whether the superintendent is hired on a permanent or interim
basis. That is, a board is more likely to want an interim superintendent to
come in and establish solid relationships with internal and external stakeholders, which requires excellent communication skills and political savvy.

Board members perceived that their interim superintendents performed
well in all five role categories, with the highest performance satisfaction
being in the areas of business management and political statesmanship
(both with $M = 4.4$). Effective communicator came in a close third, with
the mean for perceived success in this role being $M = 4.2$. Perceived
success was good in the last two categories, applied social scientist and
instructional leader ($M = 3.8$; $M = 3.6$). These results showed a ranked
perceived success level commensurate with the ranked perceived importance of each role.

Table 10.2 illustrates the perceived role importance and the perceived
role success as indicated by interim superintendents.

Interim superintendents perceived effective communication and political
statesmanship as the most important roles for an interim superintendent ($M
= 4.6$; $M = 4.2$), followed closely by business management ($M = 3.8$). The
least important roles as perceived by interim superintendents in their own
work were those of instructional leader and applied social scientist ($M = 3.6$;
$M = 3.2$). It would appear that interim superintendents have a high level of

Table 10.2. Interim Superintendent Rating: Interim Superintendents (N = 10)

	Perceived Role Importance	Perceived Role Success
Instructional Leader	3.6	3.6
Business Manager	3.3	3.8
Political Statesman	4.2	4.2
Applied Social Scientist	2.9	3.2
Effective Communicator	4.8	4.6
TOTAL MEAN	**3.72**	**3.88**

agreement with board members regarding the relative importance of each role in the interim superintendent position. That is, interim superintendents likely understand that their role as a short-term, transitional leader is different from the role of a permanent superintendent; hence less emphasis on instructional leadership and more emphasis on communication and political engagement. Interim superintendents perceived that they performed well in all five role categories, with the highest performance satisfaction being in the areas of political statesmanship and effective communicator ($M = 4.6$; $M = 4.2$). Business management came in a close third, with the mean for perceived success in this role being $M = 3.8$. Perceived success was reasonably good in the last two categories, applied social scientist and instructional leader ($M = 3.2$; $M = 3.6$).

Interestingly, when rating perceived performance, interim superintendents rated themselves slightly lower than did the board members in every category except effective communicator. This finding contrasts with the permanent superintendent perceptions of their own performance as presented in chapter 2, in which permanent superintendents rated themselves higher than their board. The area of effective communicator was the one area in which superintendents, whether interim or permanent, consistently rated themselves higher than their boards.

INTERVIEW RESULTS

Results of interviews with the ten interim superintendents and ten board members revealed several interesting observations. The key lessons from these interviews are presented below:

- Seven of ten interim superintendents said the title was helpful in fulfilling their job responsibilities; however, the interim superintendents reported that there was a different quality to their interaction with key stakeholder groups than they had as regular superintendents.
- The interim superintendents reported a lack of interaction with stakeholders, which can lead to isolation and a perceived lack of visibility.
- Even though two interim superintendents reported having no formal community involvement, four attended school activities, and four were involved in a referendum process.
- Eight of ten interim superintendents reported being very comfortable filling the roles asked of them.
- Nine of ten reported making difficult decisions on sensitive issues.
- One interim superintendent reported working more hours than as a regular superintendent, while six reported working significantly fewer hours than a regular superintendent.
- Two of ten interim superintendents stated that they could have helped with technology issues but were not asked.
- One interim stated that he or she could have helped with the superintendent search, but was not asked.
- With only three of the ten interim superintendent participants being formally evaluated by the board, there was no formal documentation of whether the interim superintendents fulfilled the roles assigned by the board of education.
- Six of ten interim superintendents stated that there was a need to clearly define role expectations for the interim superintendent and for the board to communicate specifics of the interim superintendent role with the interim superintendent.
- Two of ten stated that a board could consider using the same process that was used to hire the permanent superintendent when hiring an interim superintendent.

Other findings from the interviews included insight on the reasons an interim superintendent is hired. These reason included the timing of the permanent superintendent's departure and timeline for making a new hire, dissatisfaction with the candidate pool, and/or a desire to restructure administrative responsibilities.

Interviewees were also asked about the positive aspects of having an interim superintendent in place. The positives aspects included having more time to do a thorough search instead of rushing to hire a regular superintendent, providing the board time to review the vision and goals, and enabling the interim superintendent to provide the board with valuable and honest feedback without fear of losing his or her regular position. While it may seem prudent to have the interim superintendent involved in hiring the next superintendent, based on the interim superintendents' experiences with the hiring process, only four of the ten interim superintendents were involved in the hiring process for the next permanent superintendent.

GENERAL SUGGESTIONS/RECOMMENDATIONS

The research resulted in the following specific suggestions/recommendations for board members and interim superintendents. First, districts should have a leadership transition plan to replace a superintendent. This plan can be developed with the interim superintendent and, in most cases, sample plans are available from state school board and superintendent associations.

State associations should, can, and do provide support for boards and superintendents in filling an interim position. Many associations have a list of candidates available to fill interim superintendent positions.

Second, many board members believe that hiring an interim superintendent is the same as filling a regular superintendent vacancy. This belief must be clearly communicated to the interim superintendent along with the specific job description for the interim superintendent separate from a permanent superintendent job description.

A third finding for boards concerns the importance of clearly defining expectations of the role and the amount and style of communication expected of the interim superintendent. Interims must be clear in their acceptance of roles and the style, type, and amount of communication expected. This finding may be the most important component in the board and interim superintendent relationship.

Fourth, boards are encouraged to view an interim placement as a "positive opportunity," then step back and reflect on what they learn. Their insights can be useful in hiring a permanent superintendent because they will have the benefit of the interim superintendent's perspective and will have had an opportunity to work under a different model than their previous superintendent.

Finally, both boards and interim superintendents should address the five roles during an interim placement (instructional leader, business manager, political statesman, applied social scientist, and effective communicator). It is critical that the board and interim superintendent support one another during the interim superintendent's tenure and transition to a new permanent superintendent. All of the work of the interim superintendent must be strategic and agreed upon.

Once the new, permanent superintendent is hired, the board and the interim superintendent must commit to the new leader. An interim can serve as a valuable resource for the permanent superintendent during a brief period of transition. To make the transition smooth, the interim superintendent must be supportive, yet dispensable; the board must be willing to let go of the interim superintendent and move forward with the permanent superintendent.

REFERENCES

Black, S. (2009). The interim CEO. *American School Board Journal, 196*(4), 53–54.

Cook, G. (2006). Comings and goings: The fine art of superintendent transitions. *American School Board Journal, 193*(2), 14–17.

Dye, C., Fairley, D., and Otto, K. (2008). CEO transition and succession. *Trustee, 61*(8), 7–10.

Johnson, M. C., and Douglas, J. R. (1990, May). Grow your own: A model for selecting administrators. *NASSP Bulletin, 74*(526), 34–38.

Kowalski, T., McCord, R., Peterson, R., Young, I. P., and Ellerson, N. (2010). *The American school superintendent: 2010 decennial study*. Lanham, MD: Rowman and Littlefield.

Sanacore, J. (1997) Interim superintendents: Select with care. *Education Week, 16*(26), 37.

Vollendorf, J. R. (2012) *Perceptions of interim superintendent job expectations*. Doctoral dissertation. Madison, WI: Edgewood College.

11

Resources, Books, Articles, Dissertations, and Summary of Selected Research

There are many informative and helpful resources for school board members and superintendents to study and utilize. This chapter lists the references used or considered for use in this book and provides an extensive, but not exhaustive, list of the many resources available to board members and superintendents.

BOOKS

Alsbury, T. L. (2008). *The future of school board governance: Relevancy and revelation*. Lanham, MD: Rowman and Littlefield Education.

Badaracco, J. (2002). *Leading quietly*. Boston: Harvard Business School Press.

Bass, B. M., and Stogdill, R. M. (1990). *Stogdill handbook of leadership: A theory and research* (2nd ed.). New York: Free Book.

Bernes, L. V., and Nardite, D. (1999). *The sixteen personality types: Descriptions for self-discovery*. Hollywood: Radiance House.

Buckingham, M., and Clifton, D. (2001). *Now discover your strengths*. New York: Free Press.

Burbach, M. E., Barbuto, L. E., and Wheeler, D. (2003). *Linking an ability model of emotional intelligence to transformational leadership behaviors*. 46th Annual Midwest Academy of Management Meeting. St. Louis, MO, April 3–5.

Burns, J. M. (1978). *Leadership*. New York: Harper and Row.

Collins, J. (2001). *Good to great*. New York: Harper Collins Publishers.

Council for Chief State School Officers. (1996). *Interstate school leaders' licensure consortium: Standards for school leaders*. Washington, D.C.

139

Deal, T. E., and Peterson, K. (1999). *Reframing the path to school leadership.* Thousand Oaks, CA: Corwin Press.

Eadie, D. (2005). *Five habits of high impact school boards.* Lanham, MD: Scarecrow Education.

Evert, T. F., and Van Deuren, A. E. (2012). *Making external experts work: Solutions for district leaders.* Lanham, MD: Rowman and Littlefield.

Evert, T. F., and Van Deuren, A. E. (2013). *Thriving as a superintendent: How to recognize and survive an unanticipated departure.* Lanham, MD: Rowman and Littlefield Education and American Association of School Administrators.

Fullan, M. (2008). *The six secrets for change: What the best leaders do to help their organizations survive and thrive.* San Francisco: Jossey-Bass.

Glass, T. E., Björk, L., and Brunner, C. C. (2001). *The study of the American superintendency, 2000: A look at the superintendent of education in the new millennium.* Arlington, VA: American Association of School Administrators.

Glass, T. E., and Franceschini, L. A. (2007). *The state of the American school superintendency: A mid-decade study.* Lanham, MD: Rowman and Littlefield Education.

Hoffman, E. (2002). *Psychological testing at work.* New York: McGraw-Hill.

Keane, W. G., and Moore, D. (2001). *The disappearing superintendent applicant: The invitation to apply goes unanswered.* In C. C. Brunner and L. Björk (Eds.), *The new superintendency: Advances in research and theories of school management and educational policy* (Vol. 6). Kidlington, Oxford, UK: Elsevier Science Ltd.

Kolb, D. (1984). *Experiential learning: Experience as the source of learning and development.* Englewood Cliffs, NJ: Prentice-Hall.

Kowalski, T. J. (2006). *The school superintendent: Theory, practice, and cases* (2nd ed.). Thousand Oaks, CA: SAGE Publications.

Kowalski, T. J., McCord, R. S., Peterson, G. J., Young, I. P., and Ellerson, N. (2011). *The American school superintendent: 2010 decennial study.* Lanham, MD: Rowman and Littlefield.

Marzano, R. J. (2009). *Formative assessment and standards-based grading: Classroom strategies that work.* Bloomington, IN: Solution Tree.

Marzano, R. J., and Waters, T. (2009). *District leadership that works: Striking the right balance.* Bloomington, IN: Solution Tree Press.

Merrill, D., and Reid, R. (1981). *Personal styles & effective performance.* Boca Raton, FL: CRC Press.

Northouse, P. (1997). *Leadership: Theory and practice.* Thousand Oaks, CA: SAGE Publications.

Rath, T., Clinton, D., and Conchie, B. (2008). *Strengths-based leadership.* New York: Gallup Press.

Rebore, W. (2011). *Human resources administration in education: A management approach*. Boston: Pearson.

Reeves, D. (2004). *Assessing educational leaders: Evaluating performance for improved individual and organizational results*. Thousand Oaks, CA: Corwin Press.

Shilts, G. W. (2006). *Guy'd Lines—Rules for living from my 30 years as a psychotherapist*, Janesville, WI: Crossroads Psychological Services, LLC.

Strauss, W., and Howe, N. (1991). *Generations*. New York: Quill.

Strauss, W., and Howe, N. (2006). *Millennials and the pop culture*. Great Falls, VA: Lifecourse Associates.

Walser, N. (2009). *The essential school board book better governance in the age of accountability*. Cambridge, MA: Harvard Education Press.

ARTICLES

Alsbury, T. L. (2014). Jefferson County Public Schools: Shaping the future. 2013 School Board Quality Standards Report.

Bhimsack, K., and McCabe, T. (2013, July/August). 7 Practices of highly effective board members. *American School Board Journal, 200*(7), 21–25.

Bind, L. (2013, July 6). A new era for school boards. *Milwaukee Journal Sentinel*, p. 13.

Black, S. (2009). The interim CEO. *American School Board Journal, 196*(4), 53–54.

Carlson, L. (2013, August 6). School board wants greater control over message, district administration. *Marshfield News Herald*, Milwaukee, WI.

Caruso, Jr., N. D. (2013). Board savvy superintendents—help the board take its own temperature. *School Administrator, 70*(6), 11.

Cook, G. (2006). Comings and goings: The fine art of superintendent transitions. *American School Board Journal, 193*(2), 14–17.

Dye, C., Fairley, D., and Otto, K. (2008). CEO transition and succession. *Trustee, 61*(8), 7–10.

Eleven tips for savvy superintendents—the communication factor in superintendent success. (2008). *National School Public Relations Association*. https://www.aasa.org/SchoolAdministratorArticle.aspx?id=14126.

Enoch, S. (2013). Board savvy superintendents: Conversing courageously with your board. *School Administrator, 70*(11), 11.

Fuqua, A. B. (2000, April) A board divine or divided: Sustaining a positive relationship. *The School Administrator*. https://www.aasa.org/SchoolAdministratorArticle.aspx?id=14126.

Iowa Association of School Boards (IASB). (2001, April). *The lighthouse inquiry: Schoolboard/superintendent team behaviors in school districts with extreme differences in students' achievement.* Paper presented at the annual meeting of the American Educational Research Association, Seattle, WA.

Johnson, M. C., and Douglas, J. R. (1990, May). Grow your own: A model for selecting administrators. *NASSP Bulletin, 74*(526), 34–38.

Kennedy, D. C. (2013, May 31). WASB director explains what makes a healthy school board. *Daily Press*, Ashland, Wisconsin.

Land, D. (2002, January). Local school boards under review: Their role and effectiveness in relation to students' academic achievement. *John Hopkins University*, Report No. 56.

Matthews, J., Floyd, D. G., Ilg, T., and Rohn, C. A. (2002). Succession: Insiders vs. outsiders. *School Administrator, 59*(5). Retrieved from http://0proquest.umi.com.oscar.edgewood.edu/.

Moscinski, D. (2013). Self-fulfilling prophecy. *American School Board Journal, 200*(6), 14–15.

Sanacore, J. (1997). Interim superintendents: Select with care. *Education Week, 16*(26), 37.

Schneider, P. (2014, May 29). Evaluating Cheatham—12 Madisonians size up the superintendent's first year on the job. *Wisconsin State Journal, Capital Times Supplement*, p. 12.

DISSERTATIONS

For this book, the following dissertations served as the basis for chapters or as references.

Rindo, R. J. (2010). *High impact district governance: Effective school board member actions and practices.* Doctoral dissertation. Madison, WI: Edgewood College.

Severson, M. (2011). *Perceptions of superintendent behaviors that influence relationships with key stakeholders including board members.* Doctoral dissertation. Madison, WI: Edgewood College.

Thompson, A. (2012). *Factors that influence a Wisconsin school board's decision to hire an internal candidate to the superintendency.* Doctoral dissertation. Madison, WI: Edgewood College.

Van Deuren, A. (2012). *School board member needs and interests regarding the content, structure, and delivery and other considerations related to school board professional development*. Doctoral dissertation. Milwaukee, WI: National Louis University.

VerDuin, J. (2011). *The relationship of leadership qualities to Wisconsin school superintendent hiring practices*. Doctoral dissertation. Madison, WI: Edgewood College.

Vollendorf, J. R. (2012) *Perceptions of interim superintendent job expectations*. Doctoral dissertation. Madison, WI: Edgewood College.

WEBSITES

EducationPlanner.org (2011). *What is your learning style?* Retrieved from http://www.educationplanner.org/students/self-assessments/learning-styles.shtml.

Hetrick, W. (1993, March). *Leadership for a time of change*. Paper presented at the Annual Conference on Creating the Quality School, Oklahoma City, OK. Retrieved from http://files.eric.ed.gov/fulltext/ED357933.pdf.

Johnson-Morgan, E. (2014, March). Dysfunctional characters often sit at the board table, by the Nonprofit Risk Management Center, www.nonprofitrisk.org.

Martin, B., Johnson, J., and Lay, M. (2002). What motivates individuals to become leaders in public and higher education? *Professional Issues in Counseling*. Retrieved from http://www.shsu.edu/piic/spring2002/indexspring02.html.

McCarthy, B. (1996). 4MAT, www.aboutlearning.com.

National School Public Relations Association (2008). *Eleven tips for savvy superintendents—the communication factor in superintendent success*. Retrieved from http://www.nspra.org/files/docs/SavvySuperintendents.pdf.

Smith, S. K., Chavez, A. M., Seaman, G. W., and Barrett, P. L. (2014). *A how to guide for digital convergence in education, blended instructional models, architecting a blended curriculum, digital learning platforms, and one-on-one learning environments*. Retrieved from https://modernteacher.com/.

About the Editors and Authors

Amy E. Van Deuren, Editor

Dr. Van Deuren holds a doctorate in educational leadership from National Louis University and a master's degree in music education and law from the University of Utah. She has experience as a high school band director, lawyer, and business owner. She served as faculty member and administrator at National Louis University before taking a position as the principal at West Allis Central High School in the West Allis-West Milwaukee School District. Dr. Van Deuren has co-authored several books on music education and educational leadership, including *Music Education Dictionary*, *Wind Talk for Woodwinds*, *Wind Talk for Brass*, *Making External Experts Work*, and *Thriving as a Superintendent*.

Thomas F. Evert, Editor

Dr. Evert received his doctorate from the University of Wisconsin–Madison in educational psychology. He served as a school psychologist, high school principal, director of student services, and superintendent in three districts in Wisconsin, and retired after serving fourteen years as a superintendent. Dr. Evert currently serves as an instructor, dissertation advisor, and dissertation liaison at Edgewood College. He co-authored two books on educational leadership, *Making External Experts Work* and *Thriving as a Superintendent*.

Bette A. Lang, Editor

Dr. Lang holds her doctorate in educational administration from Marquette University and her master's and specialist's degrees from the University of Wisconsin–Superior. She has experience as a teacher, assistant principal, middle and high school principal, director of instruction, and superintendent in six school districts in Wisconsin. She retired after serving sixteen years as a superintendent in four districts. Dr. Lang is currently an instructor, dissertation advisor, and dissertation liaison at Edgewood College.

Linda K. Barrows

Dr. Barrows holds her master's degree and PhD in curriculum and instruction from the University of Wisconsin–Madison. Following work as a teacher and researcher, she was superintendent of schools for twenty-six years in three Wisconsin districts. In retirement she teaches and advises doctoral students in educational leadership at Edgewood College and works with student teachers in Cuernavaca, Mexico. She and her husband, Richard, have two daughters and four granddaughters and enjoy spending time with family, traveling, and outdoor activities.

Pamela Kiefert

Dr. Kiefert is retired, having recently served as director of student achievement and professional development and superintendent of schools. She holds a doctorate in educational leadership from Edgewood College with a dissertation titled *The Role of the Executive Director of Student Achievement in Supporting the Self-Efficacy of Principals as Instructional Leaders.*

Michele L. Severson

Dr. Severson holds a doctorate in educational leadership from Edgewood College. Her research focused on quantifying personality traits that are most effective at building positive relationships within the schools, school board, and business community. She currently serves as the district administrator of the school district of Black River Falls, Wisconsin. Through her past experiences, Dr. Severson consistently places a high priority on the tenets of servant leadership and values mutual trust as the foundation by which all relationships operate. She has worked in the school district of Black River Falls as a teacher, principal, and now as the district administrator. Dr. Severson presents at various conferences on topics such as highly effective collaboration and professional learning communities. Dr. Severson is married with two teenage sons who are heavily involved in sports—most free time is spent in the bleachers cheering them on!

Annette Van Hook Thompson

Dr. Van Hook Thompson holds a doctorate in educational leadership from Edgewood College. Her research examined factors that influence a school board's decision to hire an internal candidate to the superintendency. Dr. Thompson currently serves as superintendent of the Dodgeland School District in Juneau, Wisconsin. After obtaining her master's and educational specialist's degrees from Miami University in Oxford, Ohio, Dr. Thompson worked as a school psychologist in Ohio, Hawaii, and Wisconsin. Additionally, she has served as a district assessment coordinator, district gifted and talented coordinator, and at-risk student intervention program manager.

Joel A. VerDuin

Dr. VerDuin holds a doctorate in educational leadership from Edgewood College. His research focused on the relationship of leadership qualities to superintendent hiring practices. Dr. VerDuin currently serves as the chief technology and information officer in the Anoka-Hennepin School District, Minnesota's third largest school system. Professional interests include organizational improvement and strategic planning with a focus on how to use technologies to provide more relevant and authentic experiences for students. His past experience in education includes detention supervisor, middle school teacher, network engineer, and various versions of technology director-level positions. Hobbies, aside from spending time with his family, include home-brewing beer.

Jon R. Vollendorf

Dr. Vollendorf holds a doctorate in educational leadership from Edgewood College. His research focused on the perceived job expectations of interim superintendents. Dr. Vollendorf is currently serving as the principal at Stevens Point Area Senior High in Stevens Point, Wisconsin. He recently completed his twentieth year in education and has served as an English teacher, basketball coach, high school assistant principal, and district director of secondary education, and junior high school principal.